Contents

The Success Quotient

How to Capitalize on YOUR OWN Hidden Formula

By C.K. Murray

Copyright © 2018 C.K. Murray

All Rights Reserved

Join the Newsletter

Similar works by C.K. Murray:

Master Mind: Unleashing the Infinite Power of the Latent Brain

Body Language Explained: How to Master the Power of the Unconscious

Neuro-Linguistic Programming Explained: Your Definitive Guide to NLP Mastery

The 7 Laws of Fear: How to Make Your Deepest Insecurities Your Greatest Strengths

<u>The Stress Fallacy: Why Everything You Know Is WRONG</u>

<u>DOMINATE - How Psychopaths Think, Act and Succeed</u>

It's inside you.

Deep inside you. So far inside you, you never even knew to look. You overlooked, you underestimated, and now you're wondering if, when, how it will ever come to be.

Frankly, you had your chance. But, you *did not* blow it.

Least not yet. You can still do it. You can do better than do it, you can maximize it. Optimize it. Because unbeknownst to you, buried within the very thing that makes you, *you…* embedded in the genetic, epigenetic and protected nature of who you are, it lies...

It resides in the nooks and crannies. You've used it, but only once. Or twice. Definitely not enough. You've harnessed it at times, not even knowing. You've elevated at times, barely understanding.

And that's too bad. Because *you*, with all your faults and features, are not enough.

You *could be* so much more…

In the pages that follow, you will learn why you are lacking. You will learn how you are lacking. You will learn when

you are lacking. And most importantly of all, you will learn
the path to discovering your Personal Blueprint for
achievement and success.

What's success?

It ain't money. Sure, it can be money, but it's not about
money. It's not about the size of your house or your annual
income. How well you wine & dine, where you go on
vacation, or the car you drive, or the rich friends you hang
with, or the career you have, or the nice area of this world
you inhabit.

Success, *real* success, is about you. How. You. Feel.

About you. It's about an understanding of what you want
from this life and why you want it. But most importantly, it's
about what you do to get it.

See, many people can get… 'things.' We can all get things.
We can blow money on things, we can spend money we
don't have through credit on things, we can save and save
and finally splurge on some things, and, if we're lucky and
skilled, we can make a fortune. Then powerfully, easily
acquire more *things*.

Yet still, it's not enough, never enough. For some of us with all the things in the World, it's never, ever enough to feel good. And everywhere we look and think to look, we find: the World is filled with things. Life, is overrun with things.

Yet Life, was never about these *things*.

When you realize this, you realize everything. Do you want to cherish things? Or do you want to cherish Life? Well, your first question is, what is Life? What gives meaning to Life, and how do you give life to Meaning?

Confused?

Don't be. The key to understanding life and enjoying life, is understanding and enjoying *you*. Before you can ever conceivably understand your Personal Success Quotient, you must understand you. You must embrace *you* and love *you*. You must excuse and accept the many errors and mistakes you will make (and you will make many), and you must excuse and accept the many errors and mistakes others will make *toward* you.

You are you, they are they. And all of you taken together, no matter what you think, feel or do, are *human*.

And this is the first step, the first small but crucial stepping stone, toward *Adaptive Ascension*...

Adaptive Ascension – Defining the Ability to Overcome

What's this you ask? What does this fancy-sounding term really mean?

Well to be quite honest, it's nothing really. Just the *single* biggest factor in your ability to either fall or stand, swim or drown, thrive or die, in this wide, daunting – but rewarding – thing called Life.

Adaptive Ascension is the ability to counteract challenges. It's about seeing barriers and scaling them. It's about circumventing them. Outsmarting them. Outworking them. Outperforming them. And sometimes, it's about plowing right straight on through them.

Adaptive Ascension is about the climb. Now, that doesn't mean you won't fall, at times. Sometimes you'll even hit rock bottom. You'll lose a loved one, end up in serious medical trouble, lose money, a business, a home, a way of life you thought you knew and had, comfortable and safe, for the foreseeable future. The fact is, we all end up screwed at one point or another. And we all end up feeling incapable, for some time or another.

The difference is, some of us rise. While others fall and settle.

Adaptive Ascension requires that you never stay down. There will be dips in your life path. The *Ideal* Trajectory is never perfectly aligned with the *Real* Trajectory. You must learn to prepare for the future and to manage it accordingly. But most importantly, you must learn to manage… you.

But how?

If you're like the typical person, the average, everyday, mediocre person, then you're lacking. You wake up in the morning, more tired than you'd like to be, probably not overly excited to start your day, and certainly not radiating confidence in everything you know you need to do. More likely than not, you've got a case of <u>chronic cognitive malaise</u>. You may be wondering why you can't just snap out of bed like some people. Why you can't be more happy, more motivated, feeling loose and limber and ready to go.

In some ways, you simply don't know. Even if you do feel at least content, you know it's not good enough. You want more, but you don't know what. Part of you feels empty. A part of you feels cold and dark. You know you need, want, crave something new – but what?

Should you pursue it? Is it worth it? Or is it better to continue on the same ol' track, hoping that maybe one day things will change and life will flourish?

Do you have a plan—do you even want one?

See, when it comes to your Ideal Trajectory and Real Trajectory, you must recognize one simple but crucial truth: most people don't *have* one.

Most average, ordinary people have some vague notion of what they'd like to be doing, feeling, and how they'd like to be living, but they don't have the *trajectory* to get there.

Heck, most people can't even describe their *current* trajectory. In other words, what is actually happening? Are you on the path toward a promotion at work? A new job? Moving to a new location? Are you seeking to land a girlfriend or boyfriend, find a new partner, or take a relationship to the next level? Or are your goals simpler and more defined? Such as, say, buy a used car under a certain $$ amount? Or lose 15 lbs by summer? Or save enough money for a brief vacation with family and friends?

Whatever your trajectory, whatever your time frame, you must define it and you must record it. Chart it, track it, and most importantly, revise it.

Because, as we all know, Life is never a smooth ride.

Life Snapshot – Setting the Parameters for Trajectory

Here's what you do. First, devise your Ideal Trajectory. It doesn't have to be a lifetime plan. It can be a 5 year plan. A 5 month plan. Heck, if you're a really bad planner, it can a 5-day plan! The point is this: you are thinking ahead. Better yet, you are thinking ahead with a clarity and focus you didn't realize you had.

Give yourself time. Find a weekend or weekday to chill and ponder. Discuss with people you trust like friends and family, to determine what it is you want. But remember, it's what *you* want. Input from others is good, but ultimately this is your life. Detach from everybody if need be. Go for a long solo walk in the woods, or a run, or isolate yourself in your bedroom or basement or place of study. Sit in a coffee shop in a quiet corner.

Whatever you do, allow yourself time and space to detach. You want to reconnect with your internal voice. And the only way to do this is to remove yourself from the voices and opinions of those who are most influential. Allow the opinions of others to soften in your head, like a distant echo. Pay them heed, but do not let them dominate. Instead, weigh your own internal words. Be mindful. Use <u>the teachings of</u> <u>Theravada</u> if need be.

What matters is that you are thinking about a specific and targeted *time frame* of your life.

Now put thought to paper.

Once you have physically written or drawn your trajectory, be sure to include the following: short term goals, goal deadlines, and the ultimate outcome.

But remember. You can't possibly reach your goals without also having the resources to reach those goals. So take note. Jot down some of the things you will require to achieve your desired outcomes in the time frame you've chosen. Remember, this is merely a rough approximation. You do not need to go into excruciating detail. The purpose of this exercise is to get you thinking more seriously, while generally recognizing the constraints you face.

Here is a brief example of a rough Ideal Trajectory.

*{Week 1 –don't eat out------- *save $50*}*

*{Week 2 –don't eat out------- *save $75*}*

*{Week 3 –drive less------- *save $25*}*

*{Week 4 –no online purchases------- *save $55*}*

*{Week 5 –reduce mall shopping------- *save $60*}*

*{Week 6 –go to dollar store------- *save $45*}*

<u>End Goal: Save $310 for new bike</u>

Now of course, this is a very basic model. And your own trajectory may have nothing to do with $$ at all. Perhaps you want to further your education, talk more with your loved ones, travel somewhere for vacation, exercise more, improve health and well-being, eat better foods, or achieve something else that is not easily quantified.

Whatever you want, you want it because you think it's important. Maybe you think it will make you happy, or happier. Perhaps you simply think it will make your life easier. Or maybe, simply, it's something you've always wanted. You don't quite know why, and frankly you don't care. You just know, in your heart of hearts, that it's *good*.

So good. Don't overthink it. Once you have devised your rough Ideal Trajectory, step back. Now put that trajectory somewhere visible. Pin it on the fridge, on your bedroom wall, anywhere you can see it, and be reminded of it. Let it become a part of your daily vision. A mantra that carries you onward. Bring it into your heart, your soul, but don't obsess. Let it become a part of your subconscious. Accept it. Welcome it. Know that it is an inseparable part of what makes *you*, you. That it drives you. And that you, with all your faults and problems, are in the driver's seat.

Now give it time. When enough time has passed, however much you allotted for your Ideal Trajectory, take a seat. Find a comfortable spot, maybe with a little background noise, maybe during a quiet soft spring day. Find a place to sit, relax, and most importantly, think.

And analyze. Take a good hard look at your rough Ideal Trajectory. Now, it is time to devise your Real Trajectory. Compare what you planned to do, and what you actually did. Did you accomplish your goal and/or goals? Did you fall short? How short? Was it too hard, or were you too lazy?

Did you not care as much as you thought? Did you care too much? What held you back? And why, oh why, did you allow it to?

Truth is, most of us will fail. We will plan to reach a certain outcome, only to find it was too difficult. Or, we will set our goals so low, that when we do reach a certain outcome, we're not satisfied. We're underwhelmed, we're unimpressed. We feel like we did nothing at all.

Others may encourage us, they may congratulate us. But we won't hear it. Instead, we'll beat ourselves up. Time and time again, for just… not... being… good *enough*. Whatever it was we did, we think, was just not good enough.

And it shouldn't be. It should never be good *enough*. But that doesn't mean you should beat yourself up over it. If anything, this means you're growing. You're becoming better. You want more of yourself, you demand it.

See, the key to Adaptive Ascension is incremental steps. You have to step and skip before you can leap. With each small 'win' or success, you come closer. You adjust your focus and your goals. You shoot higher, you aim skyward. All the while, keeping your feet firmly rooted on the ground.

That is to say, in *reality*. You have to be realistic. Loving and encouraging yourself for small successes, while keeping your fire alive and raging. And this all comes down to one important conception….

The BIG FOUR

The Big Four refers to four attributes that make us tick. If there's one thing the so-called experts, gurus and motivational leaders agree on, it's this: Know Thyself.

The NUMBER ONE reason many of us fail to align out trajectories in a way that is satisfying but also challenging is this: we don't know.

We don't know who we are or where we're going. We haven't taken the time, serious time, to probe our inner depths. We have to be honest. But more importantly, we have to be *courageous*. Frankly, most people don't have the courage to look inside. Really inside. They might admit faults and insecurities here and there, feel bad about *this* or not so good about *that*, but when it comes right down to it, they're lacking.

Probing your inner depths means removing from yourself, even as you dive inside yourself. This may seem like a conundrum, but in reality it's completely true.

When we truly take the time to understand ourselves, we have to be objective. We have to look at ourselves, examine our thoughts, feelings, attitudes and behaviors in full. As if they aren't even ours...

We have to evaluate the ins and outs. This is what we call *'meta-cognition.'* This term refers to the ability to think about your thinking. To understand your understandings.

Start simple. Ask yourself why you do things the way you do.

Do you react positively in some situations and negative in others? What are you thinking and feeling when you do something negative? What are you thinking and feeling when you do something positive?

Be honest. Let's say, you drink too much sometimes. What is your thought process? When you overdo it, do you tell yourself that you're going to control yourself, only to fail? Are you knowingly lying to yourself? Or how about with overeating, or let's say, procrastinating?

Why do you repeatedly tell yourself one thing when the outcome is almost *always* the opposite?

Do you regret the way you've acted toward others? Toward a certain somebody? Why do you regret it? Better yet, why do you act that way? Do you approach that person with anger? With resentment? With the intent to hurt? With neglect? What do you tell yourself? Do you try to justify it?

Are you rationalizing your bad behaviors? Excusing your bad attitudes only to feel guilty later?

And how do you deal with this guilt? Do you binge? Do you do things that are bad for your body and brain, to somehow, subconsciously punish yourself?

<u>Now think about the positives</u>

Let's say you do something that is objectively 'good.' Maybe you volunteer at a soup kitchen. Maybe you help somebody financially in desperate need. Maybe you do everything in your power to be a good friend, to raise good kids, to be a good partner or spouse.

Consider what you think and feel when doing these positive acts…

Are you doing them because you like the feeling? Are you doing them because you feel that nobody else will? Are you doing these positive things because you feel you have to balance out the negatives? Is it a compensatory mechanism?

Why do you do these things? Why do you think these thoughts? And why do you feel these feelings?

Examine the process. What is your beginning thought? Does it create a feeling in your body? When it's positive, does your heart flutter? Do you feel warmth in your face? Can you not help, but to smile, to think that life is getting better and better?

How about when things are negative. What is your first thought? Do you think *'Screw it'*? Do you think *'I'll show them'*?

What is your physical response? Do you get a pit in your stomach or a tightness in your head or chest? Do you feel a sudden compulsion to yell, run, hide or withdraw?

Why? And if you don't like these thoughts and feelings, why do you continue to feed them?

Your mind is your body. And this *biofeedback loop* hinges on one thing.

And we call that thing, self-control. If you can learn to control your emotional reaction, you can control your physical reaction. This creates a loop in which your body is at ease, so your mind too stays at ease. Thus, you have a positive thought – so you feel good. You don't tense, you loosen. You don't grimace, you smile. Your thoughts remain positive – *'this is nice, I can do this, I like this, things are good'* – and your body follows suit. You don't feel the stress, your blood pressure doesn't rise, your head doesn't ache, and you don't feel like somebody is sitting on your back and chest.

You <u>must</u> tell yourself, in your head, what you want to happen. Next time you think you're about to blow up in anger, feel stricken with fear, or experience harsh feelings toward someone or something, tell yourself what you want to happen. What *will* happen. Explain it to yourself.

'I really don't like that,' you might say internally. *'I don't like it at all but I'll be fine. I won't lash out or act irrationally. I won't let this get to me. I'll take a breath and count to 20 and not let this get to me.'*

Becoming more positive, becoming more powerful in your own skin, is about taking ownership of your emotions.

<u>Emotional intelligence</u> is the key to this incredible transformation, and is the reason that many people – while not the smartest or the most knowledgeable – can obtain incredible success.

If you understand yourself, you can change yourself for the better. And if you can change yourself for the better, you can also change those around you. In short, you can change your *world*.

The use of certain thoughts to create certain feelings and behaviors is nothing new. It is a linguistic blueprint that literally, structurally rearranges the meanings and symbols of your reality. This <u>programmatic personalization</u> is especially powerful because it can actually *save* you life. It can reduce stress, sharpen your focus and memory, and improve the general functioning and well-being of your body and brain.

Take the following example:

You get stuck in traffic. Instead of getting worried like you used to, you now shake your head. Maybe you laugh. Maybe you groan. But you aren't mad, *real* mad. You feel thankful that you didn't get in an accident. You remind yourself that somebody could be seriously injured. At the least, have a damaged vehicle. You remember the time you had to spend too much $$ on your *own* car. You empathize.

You're running late, but you're okay. You tell yourself how you'll make up for that lost time in other ways...

Or how about this one:

You catch a cold or sickness. Instead of freaking out about how terrible you feel and how you can't do what you have to, you feel thankful. At least it's happening now and not at a more important time. You tell yourself that positive thinking actually has an <u>immunomodulatory</u> response. You realize that by *accepting* the sickness, you are already farther along the path to recovery than if you *rejected* it. You accept that you are sick, and you move ahead by providing your body and mind the fluids, food and rest required.

So there you have it. These are just two instances, but in both the trick is to understand yourself first, and your new self, *second*. Your Current Self and your Future Self.

You aspire to become better. You plan to become better. You tell yourself that you are becoming better. You think it, you feel it, you believe it, and you become it. Not overnight. Not in a week. But slowly, and surely.

Okay. So without further ado, let's... get… Right. Down. To it.

Here are the FOUR Major Attributes of your Life you <u>must</u> transform to Achieve Your Potential:

(1) 'People Skills'

Think of the world today. We live in a day and age saturated with information. Thousands of television shows, streaming services, computers, laptops, tablets and gadgets. Virtually anybody, anywhere in the world can now connect into a shared shapeless network and communicate with someone, somewhere, in a completely different part of the planet. There are so many options, so many forms of information consumption, data access, and stimulation for our fevered minds. We live in a world that is interconnected unlike ever before, yet also, perhaps, as chaotic as any before. Maybe that's why ADHD diagnoses are exploding…

But think of it. We live in a world with a million options. Which is why people need help. We all do. We need guidance, structure. We need something to do with our daily lives, a place to work, a time for fun, a way to live and sustain and pay those oh-so-lovely bills we can't avoid. We require channels, for connecting with others, times and locations for meeting our friends, loving our families.

Put simply, the modern person needs a modern solution. And that solution requites structure.

And providing that structure, depends on *you*.

In order to succeed, to reach your dreams and love your life, you need to provide structure. Not only for yourself and your daily demands, but for the people around you. This is why so-called 'people skills' are so important.

People skills are ultimately about equilibrium. You can't do what you want all the time. As much as we'd all love to cut work and obligations, to throw duties to the wind, shoot off to the beach or woods for a weekend or summer or winter (or forever), as much as we'd love to just say *'screw it'*-- we can't.

When it comes to utilizing people skills, you have to know this. You must, at all times, balance restricting influences with expanding influences. Give people something to do, a thing to work for, a feeling to hold on, a sense of order, a sense of belonging. But at the same time, give them what they desperately, humanly, *crave*.

Allow them to Soar from time to time. Give them a sense of uniqueness, compliment them, notice them, let your friends and family and even random acquaintances know you *see* them, in all their faults and glory, making their efforts to change.

Thing is, people need to feel they have a purpose. And it needs to be clear. But they also need to feel something outside that purpose. People need time to be *human*. And that means fooling around, having fun, chilling, laughing, relaxing – even doing stupid, silly stuff and making mistakes.

We all need time and room to blow off steam. We all need a way to love our lives outside of the daily structure and balance that pays our bills and keeps our homes and sustains our ways.

We have to win. We have to succeed. And most of all, we have to know, how to work with people.

<u>But how *do* we work with people?</u>

Unfortunately, there is no easy answer. But there is an answer. And believe it or not, it might be far simpler than you originally thought. Sure, people are different. Values and priorities differ. Ideologies may oppose. Thoughts and feelings may collide. But what matters, is not what these people think, feel or do individually.

What matters is what they think, feel and do, together.

Synergy.

The truth of synergy is that people will work best together when they share a common goal. A vision. A reason to put aside differences and enhance similarities.

People are strongest when they know they need each other. When they realize, despite ego, that they cannot possibly achieve success without each other.

If you want to unlock your own potential, you must first unlock the potential of others.

Become the sealant. Become the cushion. But better yet, become the leader.

In order to become a *transformational* leader that gets along with people and gets people to get along with each other, you must first get to *know* people.

So get to know them. Connect, one-on-one with the people in your life. Practice with strangers. Notice the glint in the eye of the cashier at the supermarket. Maybe she's tired and had a long day. Maybe her boss just chewed her out, and it's something you can understand, and so you make a small comment, or ask her how she's doing, or simply nod and say, *"long day, huh?"*

Notice the body language of people in passing. In the mall, coworkers, at a store, walking around a community park or recreational facility. At a restaurant, in line at a movie theater or sports venue or some other public place. Strike up conversation.

Sharpening our interpersonal skills with strangers is the best way to sharpen our overall people skills. Enhance your emotional intelligence by understanding how others feel, think and behave.

But always, *always*, look someone in the eye. Notice if they look back. Do they shy away? Do they divert their eyes, look around, then look back? Do they look back immediately? How long do they hold the stare? When do they blink?

Are their eyes glassy? Glazed? Pale? Are they bright and clear? Do people look full of life and energy? Do they look drained and lifeless? Or do they show nothing?

Think about how you might feel.

People are just like you. They have daily problems. They have dreams, they have failures. They feel bad sometimes without knowing why. Other times, they feel so good and never want it to end. They may come from completely different walks of life, of all types from all parts of this wide weird World.

But they're all the same. We're all United by our <----SHARED----> Humanity.

So think about people, especially those you don't know. Maybe they're having a bad day. Maybe their parents are sick or somebody they love just died. Or maybe they're happy, got good news on a house, or just landed a new job.

Or maybe it's just another normal, 'okay' day in a long string of mediocre times.

Make small talk. Notice what someone is wearing. Initiate with a smile and drop a comment. If it's good weather, maybe mention that. If somebody seems to be uncomfortable or anxious, acknowledge that you feel the same. If somebody is walking the dog, stop and offer a hand for a lick or to pet. Recognize that people are just people.

No different than you and I.

Be natural, never force. And never feel discouraged if you get blown off. It doesn't mean you did something wrong.

There are numerous reasons why this may happen. Maybe the other person is lost in his or her head. Or he or she simply isn't fleeing good, and isn't up to engaging. Have sympathy and empathy, not antipathy and acrimony. In other words, understand that someone else might be feeling down, and be okay with it. Accept it. Perceive it, but don't judge it.

And if you feel so inclined, do something about it…

"How are you?" "How's it going?" "You need any help?" "You okay?" "How ya feeling?" "Hey, everything okay?"

Making a simple but meaningful gesture such as these can go a long way. Especially coming from a stranger.

Now. Move onto the people you know.

This will be harder in some ways and easier in others. It's hard because you know these people better and will have a whole host of complicated feelings and thoughts concerning them. However, it will be easier because you *do* know them, and have talked to them in deeper more meaningful terms.

The best way to deal with these individuals is to keep a safe distance.

What does that mean?

Well, it doesn't mean you disconnect. Quite the contrary. What a 'safe distance' really means is that you stay away from your family, friends and so on, when it is acceptable—and necessary—to do so. In the long-term this actually *increases* connectivity.

Distance is critical to maximizing a relationship. Every expert, every research article, every study of the multifarious influences in factorial relationships will tell you: space is key.

Guys that constantly contact girls are considered beta males. They are looked upon as weak and needy, as not 'real men.' Women that contact guys too often are also seen in negative terms. They are considered neurotic or clingy, not independent and strong, but insecure and flimsy.

With families and friends, the equation is much the same. You don't need to reach out to someone all the time. Family members who disproportionately require contact, are viewed negatively. They are considered less autonomous, more troubled, possibly inept, and maybe even 'lost.'

Just think about how others might perceive *you*. If you are constantly reaching out, in unhealthy fashion, others will grow tired. Or worried. They might think you're obsessed. Or worse, that you don't have your own life. Or that you're struggling with something bad.

Now, if you have a drug, alcohol or serious life-circumstance problem, *Okay*. But not all family and friends will recognize this unless you make it explicit. And at a certain point, it's on you. Only you can change you. All the long talks, sit-downs, interventions, and outside efforts can only go so far.

And if you don't have a serious issue, and you just like to stay in touch—remember:

It's one thing to show caring and compassion, to stay connected and touch base. It's another thing entirely to smother a person.

Space is critical.

But you shouldn't totally detach either. Learn to know the people you are talking to. Do they prefer you to touch base often? Do they want you to let them be? Some people can pick up a conversation right where it left off after months of no contact. Others, require regular contact to know you still care and are still there.

Know your friends and family. We all have that one friend that we don't see often, but when he or she is in town, we get along like we've been together the whole time. Other friends are more frequent, we can't imagine not seeing them for months on end, and if such a thing were to happen, we're not sure the friendship would stay intact.

Everybody has different needs, at different points in Life. Some family members are better left to their own devices. Some need to see you. A lot.

So stay in touch, but never stay around for too long. You have your own life, your own dreams. Your friends have their own lives and dreams. Your coworkers have their own lives and dreams.

Accept it, respect it, and use it….

<u>To Optimize Your Strategic Gains</u>

(2) Optimizing Your Strategy

If you want to get the most out of yourself, to unlock your greatest strengths and maximize your strategic successes, you have to do a few important things. Firstly, you have to get off your butt.

Do some research.

What is your aim? And what do you want?

Think of it in terms of work. But also, think of it in terms of life.

Okay, so you want to continue in your career. Great. But what does that mean? Do you want to move laterally to a new position in a similar company? Do you want to rise in your company? Do you want to change careers? Do you merely want a raise?

Now think of life. Okay, so you want to "be a better person." What does that mean? Help out the homeless? Start a family? Be more honorable, more trustworthy, more transparent in your everyday life?

And don't forget: this is Life.

Sometimes people have trouble. Sometimes problems come out of *nowhere*. Just like opportunities. Sometimes you meet someone on the street, they make a comment, you make a comment, the two of you find some weird improbably connection or spark, and then you've got a business card, or a number, or a potential start to a new way of life.

Or maybe just a new friend…

Although things like this don't happen often, they do happen. And they illustrate an important point. Life is crazy. There are countless interrelated factors that change the way we live, dramatically and subtly.

Times change and people change, and no matter what we do, we can't stem the flood of change.

But what we can do is plan for it. Through focused, reasoned strategy.

So here are the three pillars for forming a sustained, significant strategy:

<u>A</u>. Know How to Start

Most people don't know what to do. They have some vague notion or unformed idea (*"I wanna be a writer"*) but they don't know where to begin. They don't know what education they need, what accreditation they require, who to talk to and what to see. They simply have no idea how to get off the ground and get running.

Don't be clueless.

Learn from the best. Watch the Youtube videos and learn the science. Get on it fast and on it good. Get on it like nobody's business. Think of it. For every 1,000 people that tried, many more have failed. Only some have reach consistent success, and only a small, tiny fraction of those people have reached the highest level of achievement.

If you want to be a financial guy, you have to major in finances, business or mathematics. You have to reach out to internships and vocational opportunities early. You have to have an affinity for math. Learn how to save money, start investing early. Start your own businesses early. Try, fail, try and fail. Keep learning and keep watching your money.

If your idea of success is not job or career but personal development, the starting point is important too.

Say you want to become stronger. Well what kind of strength? Do you want to be 'lean and mean'? Do you want to bulk up? Do you want to be an endurance athlete? Are you seeking mental strength? Would you like to <u>turbocharge your brain's latent abilities</u> Or unlock new methods for stress management?

Whatever kind of 'strength' you are seeking as part of your personal development regimen, do not go into it blindly. Look up the people who know, the workout and diet plans that work, the lifestyles that succeed. Understand the philosophies, and by all means, find actual research articles. One good way to do this is to Google the topic of your interest + "scholarly." So if you want to read a scientific journal article on, say., Crossfit, you could Google: "Crossfit effects scholarly" or "Crossfit program scholarly."

You gotta start somewhere in life. If you want to succeed, you need to do it the only way that works. From the beginning.

<u>B</u>. Know Where to End

Most people don't know what they're aiming for. Sure, most people want *something*, but then what? Say they get it (their ideal job, their dream home, the spouse of their dreams, a good family, a comfortable white picket suburban existence) – okay. Now what?

Are you done?

Do you retire and move to Florida? Do you say you're happy and stop? Do you call it a night?

For people who reach their 'dreams' there is always room for improvement. Even if you're young and successful and feel like the world is at your fingers, you've got more to do. Even if you're old and gnarled, you've got more to do.

Life is about living. It's about finding a reason to get up every day and press on, and live on, and enjoy the things in the world that you've fashioned for yourself and those important to you.

But what if you haven't reached your dreams? To be honest, most of us haven't. To be even more honest, a number of us won't.

Does that make you sad?

Well it shouldn't. It should drive you. It should inspire you to be an anomaly, to rise above and show everyone that you're something different.

But wait.

First you have to find out where you want to end. That's right, know your end before you begin. Remember: one end is just a new beginning. You can always start something else up... But you can only do this, once you reach closure on something else.

Think of the previous examples. If you want to prosper in a career, in finances or something else, how do you know when you've 'made it'? What do you do? Is it a senior position at corporate? Is it when you've reached a certain salary threshold or have a certain $$$ amount in your checking and savings accounts?

Or how about with the personal development realm? The Crossfit example…. When are you 'done' and ready to start a new plan? Do you want to be able to complete a full workout? Do you want to reach a certain weight, have a certain muscle density, be able to do a certain amount of reps of a certain activity?

See, most people don't know where they want to end up. So they give up, or they look around wondering why everybody *else* seems to have it figured out.

Look at your life in terms of phases. Think of it like learning to swim. What happens first? First you approach the water. You're nervous, it's unfamiliar, you don't know what to expect. Maybe you dip in, maybe you check out the shallow end for a bit, looking far over to the deep end and wondering if you'll one day make it.

Time passes. Effort builds. And finally, maybe one day you've experienced enough that you try it out. You can doggy paddle, you can swim—a bit—and now you're ready to go deeper…

So maybe you slowly but surely swim closer to that deep-end wall day after day. Or maybe, just maybe, your plan is to dive in without fear.

So you do it.

You dive in. You're freaking out, your arms and legs are flailing. Fight or flight. Fight or flight. And so you fight, you attack, you tackle head-on the challenge in your way.

And you live. You breathe, and now you're here, having struggling, having endured, rising to the surface, not having sunk, not having drowned but having recovered.

Having *succeeded*.

Good. But now what do you do? You're young but not too young. Ready but not reckless. Experienced but not jaded. So what do you do? Where do you go?

And then you know. You pause in that water, that sea you've now conquered, and you look, beyond and outside, that lovely pool…

To a bigger pool. To a bigger place. To the wide, wild, ravaging *ocean*...

(C) Know When to Go

But what if you weren't ready for the ocean? What if instead of flailing your arms and getting to the surface and moving your legs and learning to float, you stopped? What if you had given up? What if you didn't believe it would ever work?

Would you allow yourself to drown? Would you give up the doggy paddle and sink? What would you do if the feeling began to hit, the air running out, the tightness in your chest, the darkness rushing all around, the light from the world above you fading so fast as you drifted down down down to the bottom of the dark…

Would you immediately give up? Would you allow yourself to sink, drown and die?

Of course not. But in many ways, this is what so many of us do. We don't know when to keep going. We give up before we've truly tried. And as a consequence, we allow our dreams, our visions, our goals-in-progress to *die*, before they ever truly get living.

Knowing when to keep going is about understanding that you have more to give. According to Malcolm Gladwell, it takes 10,000 hours of "deliberate practice" for you or I to become a 'world-class' expert at something. In other words, you have to spend A LOT of time if you truly want to reach your potential. Spending just an hour a day, you would need to spend 27 YEARS to become world-class level.

But maybe you don't want to be world-class (how many of us can actually do that?)

Maybe you just seek to be better. Well, the principle is the same. Don't give up! Don't give in! Some of the most successful people got that way because they refused to quit. Sure, they usually have some sort of innate ability or talent, but talent alone is not going to make you great. Michael Jordan had all the physical gifts in the world but even he had to practice something like 7 HOURS a day.

Be real with yourself. If you don't have the fire, then maybe it's not for you. There are things we will try and then there are things that burn inside us on a daily basis, that fuel our convictions and desires, and give us an underlying reason to get up in the morning.

Some things you will fall in love with. Other things, you will like from the very beginning. Sometimes you will tire of things, and sometimes, you know from the very start that it's just... Not... For you.

It's up to you, ultimately. Take the words and wisdom of others, elders and friends and families, but never let them make the decision for you. Let them offer practical advice, but never forsake your own dreams for theirs. This is your life and you have to live it. Keep an eye open for new doors and opportunities, and keep an open mind for new ideas.

Just always be honest. With yourself first, and others second. We all have to endure things we don't like, jobs we get tired with, people we'd rather not be around, places and things that are less than ideal. But in the end, what matters is that we put in the time for these things, in order to fuel what we really want.

(3) Self-management

But getting what you want requires time. It requires diligence. It requires skill. And most importantly, it requires sacrifice. It doesn't matter what it is. Whether you wanna become a circus performer, a movie star, a manager, or simply a better mother, father, son, daughter or friend. Whatever the aim, whatever the goal, you need to make sacrifice.

Sacrifice has many forms. Maybe you spend more weekends staying in and working than going out. Maybe you cut certain expenditures, or spend less time on certain activities, and spend more time around other people doing other things.

Whatever it may be that you're seeking, get to it.

One of the primary reasons people don't reach their goals is procrastination. Learning <u>adaptive strategies</u> for curbing procrastination is key. Don' t put off for tomorrow what you can do today. Consider the three components of successful self-management:

(a) Cycle Time – this concept refers to the ability to focus on the production of the product or service from its inception to its completion. In this sense, the 'product' or 'service' represents you. The new version of you, improved, with new skills, in a new position, job, career, or life situation. Think of improving yourself as you would improving something inanimate. When you write a good paper, you go through it thoroughly. You double-check, you make sure it's polished, you make sure it's good overall, but also that the details are good. When you complete a chore, or get a new car, or buy a needed item, you undergo a similar process. You check everything out, you pose questions and seek answers, and you generally ensure that everything is up to your standards.

(b) Cost Analysis – this concept refers to the 'cost' of what you're doing. What will you be giving up? Will you have to give up monetary costs? Will you be investing in new tools or resources? Will you be paying for additional education or training? Will you have to spend more to get where you hope to be, whether it's something as basic as increased gas mileage, or something bigger like having to move?

Or is the cost not monetary? Perhaps it's both monetary and non-monetary? Maybe you have to give up time doing leisure activities. Maybe you have to stop seeing certain friends as often as you would like? Maybe you have to give up old relationships, frequented places, or enjoyable habits in order to embark on your new journey?

Consider all the costs, write them down and carry them with you. Post them on your fridge. Have them in multiple places so that you are always aware. Make sure that you are okay with these changes. And if you find yourself unsure as to the balance between the costs and the benefits, consider:

(c) Quality control – this refers to the quality of the new *you*. If you're going to be making all these sacrifices, you better be getting something good in return! Are you pursuing something you've always wanted? Are you getting a higher salary, more recognition, a greater sense of daily satisfaction? Do you feel that you're finally making a noticeable improvement in the world? What is the *quality* that you have gained or improved? Are you healthier, happier, or better looking? Are you richer, safer or more secure? Ensure that the quality of your new path, lifestyle or life *exceeds* the cost of that new path, lifestyle and/or life. By how *much* it exceeds, is up to you.

Some people want to put in a little to get a lot. Some people feel *guilty* if they put in a little and get a lot. Other people don't want much, needing only a little more than they 'sacrifice' - and some people, well some people would actually rather get *less* in return, believing that the giving is more important than the getting.

It is up to you to decide who you are and what you want, and what you will do to get there.

(4) The Three Ls

Loot. Location. And Luck.

Loot, obviously is how much you have. Do you have a savings? Are you on a bare-bones budget? Do you have a decent checking account but not a good savings? Have you run up too many credit card bills? Are you in debt? Are you debt free? Are you living paycheck to paycheck? Are you comfortable?

What's your disposable income?

Then there's Location. Where are you? Where do you live? Where do you work? Do you have a long commute? Is it a nice area, a safe area? Are you in a city where everything you need is a few blocks away? Do you need a vehicle? Are you in a small town? Are you out in the country, a 30-min drive from the nearest store? Where do you live and how do you live based on it? Is your location more help or hindrance?

And finally, Luck. What's your luck like? Some people just seem lucky. They narrowly dodge disasters, they escape trouble, they find $50 bills floating in the ocean. Other people, unfortunately, always seem to land in hot water.

They have a tendency to mess up. To fall down. To fall flat on their faces, when life goes sideways. No matter what they try to do, where they happen to go, they always seem to draw a bad hand.

Are you lucky or unlucky? And when, do you wager, your luck will run out?

Consider the three Ls as a basic blueprint for your current life. You are where you are – Location. You are defined by your environment, by the people, places and things that impact your daily life. Everything from that big pothole in the road to the boss at your office that you don't like.

You are your Loot. How much money you have, how much you can get for the foreseeable future. Your bills, your expenditures, and those guilty pleasures you just can't resist. Money isn't everything but it sure makes a lot of things possible if you know how to use it.

And even more things possible, in the future, if you know how to save it.

And finally, Luck. Some people believe there is a science to luck. That the very molecules of the universe are encoded to react a certain way at a certain time, given all of our past experiences and behaviors. Sound crazy? Well, maybe it is or maybe it's not. But some people sure do seem to do better…

The question is, is Luck really Luck? Or is Luck just being smart, and resourceful, and well-coordinated? Is it just that some people do things unconsciously, or have better instincts, or minimize risk?

Some people say, what goes around comes around.

Other people? Just spinning in circles…

OKAY.

So now that we've covered some of the primary factors in your personal success, it's time to get more technical. Remember, this book is about the Success *Quotient*. For you unenlightened, non-mathematical types, that's numbers. That's formulas.

So without further ado, let's Dive. Right. In…

The Ultimate Achievement Formula

When it comes to personal success, whether in life or in business or in anything else, you have to know what you're working with. Do it, do it well, do it intelligently, and do it for a sustained, pragmatic period.

Success =

$$\frac{Effort}{Stressors \times \# \text{ of Tasks}} \quad (Ability \; x \; Access)$$

The Low

= **Success**

Now, if you (like me) are not too keen on numbers or fancy-schmancy formulas, here's the breakdown:

<u>Effort</u> – First, we must consider how much effort we are giving. Effort does not necessarily equal the efficiency of

your attempts, or the output of your activities. Effort refers strictly to how much raw 'fuel' you are burning, how much energy you are putting into reaching your vision of success. Are you getting up early and staying up late? Are you devoting more time throughout the day where before you would have goofed off or procrastinated? Are you cutting your lunch hours short? Are you doing more on weekends? How many extra hours a week are you putting in? Remember, what ultimately matters is how you are channeling this effort, applying your mental and physical energies, in a way that is sustainable. There's no point in totally busting your hump for a week till you're exhausted and then can't get back on track. Make sure your effort is balanced. And part of finding that balance? Starts with your stressors and tasks...

<u>Stressors</u> – More broadly, this refers to the many factors that affect your success. Do you have obligations to your friends and family? Do you live a hectic life? Is your diet not as good as it should be, is your sleep lacking, are you dealing with a tough family life, or crazy relatives, or too much constant stress at work? Do you drink too much or smoke too much or not exercise enough? What keeps you stressed? Do you have high blood pressure? Do you get tension

headaches? Are you in need of <u>Mindfulness-Based Cognitive Therapy (MBCT)</u>?

See if you can quantify your stressors. Think of them in order from most pressing (your daily struggles) to least pressing (occasional problems that crop up). Think about how much time worrying or focusing on each stressor you spend. Are some stressors easily remedied, but you just procrastinate? Or are your stressors not easily solved, requiring great mental, emotional and physical energy over a long duration of days, weeks, months or even years? Which stressors do you bring on yourself by your lifestyle choices, and which stressors are outside of your control (ie; death of a family member).

Determine which stressors you can limit, and which are necessary to reaching your personal vision of success.

<u># of Tasks</u> – You've probably heard the saying: *"don't put all your eggs in one basket."*

Fair enough. Don't rely solely on one thing because that one thing could always fall through. That said, don't put your eggs in a hundred baskets either. Try to find 2 – 4 main pursuits that either complement one another, or represent their own unique interests. Just make sure that these pursuits do not completely dominate your time and life, and that, you know, you can have a life outside of them. Just don't go throwing all your heart and soul into ONE thing without a back-up.

Now, we all know certain tales. Some visionary maddening genius, somewhere all secluded, spending his or her life obsessing over one thing and reaching great results in the end.

Sure it happens. But for most of us, this is not effective. Many of us will find what works and what doesn't, what we want to sustain and what we don't. So keep your number of tasks relatively low, minimize your stress and divide your effort over these two factors.

Remember the equation above. Think of this in numerical terms. Your effort is *divided* across the product of your stressors and tasks. Obviously the more stress you have, the more your tasks are compounded. Person A might be able to tackle, say, 10 tasks if there is little outside stress. Person B will struggle with just two tasks if the stress is high. Moreover, Person C might be able to tackle the 10 tasks of

Person A, despite having the high stress of Person B, if the level of sustained Effort is exceedingly high.

Remember the equation. Once you have *divided* your Effort by the *product* of your Stressors & Tasks, now it is time to *multiply* this quantity (or quality) by the *product* of Ability and Access.

Confused? Let me explain further.

<u>Ability</u> – so this refers generally to your natural aptitude. Although many people argue that ability is environmentally based, that we can change it based on our experiences, attitudes and behaviors, this is only *partly* true. Frankly, at a certain point ability stops. No matter how hard I train or try, I will never be able to run a 4 minute mile with the Kenyans. No matter how much I study, think, and learn, I will never be able to have a brain like Stephen Hawking's, or have an IQ as high as his was. At a certain point, we simply run out of real estate.

So be honest with yourself. By all means test your abilities, press your boundaries, and improve your aptitudes as much as you can, but don't lie. Some of us simply can't do things as well as other people. Sometimes it's for obvious physical reasons, other times the reasons are not easily observed.

This is why it's important to know what your strengths and weaknesses are, and to work on both. By strengthening your weaknesses, you also strengthen your strengths. Because what this does is enable you to waste less time with things that once gave you trouble, and to focus your efforts on those things you want to be doing. Most of us do things we are good at. Do we do these things because we are good at them, or are we good at them because we do them? Similarly, do we like something because we're good at it, or are we good at it because we like it and therefore we put more effort in because it doesn't feel like work?

Well, what came first: the chicken or the egg?

Point is, who really knows? And honestly, that's not what's important. If you like something, go for it. Just know that you will be better at some things, find some things easier, and find some things very difficult. Now, some of us enjoy the more difficult things. We get bored with stuff we're naturally good at and look for new avenues to challenge ourselves. This is good. It's healthy, it's productive, and it helps make us more complete, unified individuals.

So, by all means, go out there and pursue the things you like, and the things you want, even if you believe you're naturally better at other things. Just be realistic. And understand, that you should never waste time comparing your ability to another person's. You are the unique product of your genetics, experiences, environments and so on. Be *you*, and be the best you that you can be.

<u>Access</u> – Access refers to your ability to get in touch with resources. This is a wide-ranging problem that affects both individuals and groups. Consider for example people who have never seen a laptop or tablet, who rarely get access to the internet, who grow up in squalor and as a result have limited education. Now, compare to someone who has always had all these things and is able to consistently and easily derive information from search engines, news aggregates, and social media websites.

When it comes to access, everybody differs. You may have unlimited access to Netflix or Hulu whereas a friend or family member or acquaintance doesn't even have basic cable. You might live in an area where your kids can go to better schools, or perhaps you know somebody who inherited a lot of money, and although he or she doesn't live in a good area, he or she can send his or her children to good private schools.

Examples of access are endless. Just remember, it's not merely about money or social position. It can be everything from basic daily activities, places, or things that you can readily access, to greater life attainment goals that might be easier for you than for someone else. For instance, a kid with no parents and a drug-addicted guardian is likely to have reduced access to higher education for a number of reasons, when compared to a kid living in a healthy two-parent household.

Now consider the equation.

In the above equation, Access is *multiplied* by Ability. This is done because these two constructs are very interrelated. You might have more access to something because of your ability. Perhaps you are a great problem-solver, a great athlete, a great 'people person.' Perhaps you have skills that you have honed that allow you to overcome obstacles, perhaps you were taught invaluable lessons from your parents or friends that help you overcome tough barriers.

Whatever your abilities, they can actively enhance your potential access. If you have, say, an 'ability' for manipulating others, you may increase your access to higher positions in companies, to more advantageous relationships with people, and to increased monetary successes. The greater your ability for your specific pursuit or goal, the greater the multiplier that ability becomes.

Some people simply have all the opportunities in the world but squander them, or fail to apply their ability, or simply do not demonstrate significant abilities. Other people have all the ability in the world, come from terrible backgrounds with little to no access, and because of that sheer ability, find their way to soaring heights and success.

Okay. Now back to the equation. Remember, this is not going to work perfectly numerically (how do you 'quantify' effort, stress, tasks, ability, access, etc.), *but,* this will give you a clearer idea of the factors at work and how those factors interplay.

Alright. So now that we've *divided* your effort over the *product* of your tasks and stressors, we can *multiply* that total by the *product* of your abilities and access.

Now, we take that total, and divide by 'The Low.'

<u>The Low</u> – this rather ambiguous term refers to that period in your pursuit, in your new lifestyle or goal attainment process that is, well, low. Think about life, in terms of a graph. No matter what you do in life, there is a learning curve. Look at sports. Take for instance, baseball. Baseball is a loooong season. Players that come out the gates hitting .500 through 10 games still have 152 games left in the season. By contrast, the guys who are doing absolutely terrible through the beginning of the season could end up with some of the better stats by the end.

Life, like sports, is built on consistency. You can't blow out too early, you've gotta give things time. There will be dips, there will be walls you have to overcome. Many people give up prematurely. Some people work too long and too hard, trying to squeeze more out of it when the best has already passed.

So consider 'The Low.' Consider, based on the research, the point or duration whereby your progress will naturally dip, and whereby you will have to redouble your efforts to fully experience true improvement. Good things take time. We will experience all sorts of bumps and valleys and pits in the road, but if we continue on that road with the right mindset and the right skill-sets, we can continue to rise.

The details are important, but sometimes you have to step back and view the whole picture. This all ties into the previously mentioned Ideal and Real Trajectory. The Ideal Trajectory would be a continuous upward curve of progress. The Real Trajectory goes up if you're successful, but not nearly as cleanly or as clearly as we might hope.

Ultimately, 'The Low' is the denominator of this success equation because it represents the last big factor affecting our potential for success. Once all the other factors are multiplied and assessed, we have to divide that synergy, that total, that collective result, by the natural drop in progress. We have to spread our results thus far across a trajectory with a known low or valley. Once divided by The Low, you get the *Quotient*.

The Low is not the entirety of the curve, it isn't even a large part of it if you stay the course, but it is a certain and important part. It is important because it separates the doers from the pretenders. Will you stop when the going gets tough? Will you lose confidence, doubt yourself and give up? Or will you ride out the tough seas till those big waves carry you onward to new heights?

The choice is yours, lifetime traveler. The power, indeed, is truly yours.

Intrapersonal Success: The Top Power Multipliers

Okay, but what if you're tired of doing things one way. What if you want to shake things up, what if it's not merely your environment or the people in it that you want to change, but yourself included. What if you want to actually, physically restructure the building blocks of your entire *reality microcosm*?

Sound ridiculous? Sound absurd?

Well no, not exactly. And I'm not even talking about neurolinguistic programming or some ancient mystic sense of mind-body symbiosis. What I'm referring to is a very real, highly scientifically-based, evidence-supported program for change.

This is *intra*personal. There is *inter*personal, the connection between yourself and others, and then there is intrapersonal, the connection between yourself and, well, uhh.. yourself

Intrapersonal is about understanding yourself, and although we have touched on this briefly in the previous pages, now we go full-on in. If you're seeking to maximize and optimize your understanding of yourself and your faculties and your powers and your weaknesses and your insecurities and your shortcomings and your aptitudes and everything else that makes you undeniably, inexcusably, indefatigably *you*—then Intrapersonal Success is for you!

You are you. Now, let's get into what the Heck that actually means...

The 'Intelligence' Paradigm

Let's begin with the concept of 'intelligence.' For this, we will not be going into intelligence in the formal sense. Everybody has heard of IQ, and most people are familiar with <u>IQ-boosting exercises.</u> Similarly, most people have heard of EQ, and most people are aware of <u>EQ-boosting exercises.</u>

But what about multiple intelligences? Which intelligences are your strongest? Which do you need to work on? And how, the heck, do you even know??

Let's start with the basics. Harvard psychologist Howard Gardner first derived this theory when he found traditional conceptions of intelligence too limiting. In Gardner's mind, taking all of the factors involved in the human brain and expressing them through one numerical IQ or G-score was simply crazy.

So he developed an alternative. In his conception, intelligence equated to an ability to problem solve and create so-called "products" of importance in one or more cultures.

From that point on, thousands of scholars, psychologists, psychiatrists and specialists around the world adopted the theory and principles of Gardner to formulate their own assessments and tests. However, to this very day, Howard Gardner has yet to design a test himself.

The most well-known instrument derived from his theory is actually a series of tests known as the <u>Multiple Intelligences Developmental Assessment Scales(MIDAS™).</u>

Sign up if you dare!

But Multiple Intelligence isn't just about tests or theories. It's about lifestyles. It's about career choices. It's about educational opportunities. It's about better understanding yourself, and using that new and improved intrapersonal success for a life anew.

Let's dive right in:

Multiple Intelligence Theory has since evolved to include nine different types of intelligence. In most assessments, scales and tests, there are anywhere from ~30 to 65 questions, each one typically employing a 'Likert Scale,' which is a 4-point scale with the following choices:

o *Very often*

o *Often*

o *Sometimes*

o *Rarely*

But enough about the technicalities of the test. Let's get into those 9 intelligences…

Linguistic: This refers to the capacity to use, manipulate and apply words effectively. The capacity is important because it relates to both verbal/oral ability, and the ability to write. People with high linguistic intelligence are able to readily understand the structure of language, nuances in meaning, and the various dimensions of language, such as using language to persuade, to inform, to entertain, and to reference itself. High linguistic intelligence enables us to also memorize words and increase our vocabulary with relative ease. If you or someone you know wants to increase this type of intelligence, the best method is to read widely and deeply. Come up with tricks and shortcuts to remember bigger more complex words. Also, engage other languages. Learning Spanish or French or German are key to understanding the nuances, similarities and differences among and between linguistic barriers.

Now, if you want to take linguistic intelligence even further, you can apply it to a healthy career. Most people high in linguistic intelligence, or wishing to pursue linguistic intelligence, are tremendous copywriters, editors, journalists, lawyers, poets, writers, speakers, teachers, translators, scribes, TV & radio personalities, commentators, and voice-over artists. If any of these vocations sound interesting to you, go for it!

Logical-mathematical: This intelligence refers to the capacity to effectively use, manipulate and apply numbers and numerical values. People with high logical-mathematical intellgences are easy to spot. They can whiz through math class, they can program calculators, they assemble their own computers, and when it comes to any new gadget or technology, these tech wizards always seem to have it figured out. Most people high in this intelligence will go into STEM-related fields. They'll be mathematicians, accountants or statisticians. They'll be computer programmers, coders, even intelligence analysts.

If you or someone you know finds logic easy, if you are good at pattern recognition and understanding relationships between variables, you are likely strong in logical-mathematical intelligence. You can readily categorize, classify, infer and generalize. You can calculate and you can reason, and when it comes to taking numbers and making sense of them, few can do it better.

So go forward into the world! Enjoy those numbers and equations and help explain this crazy thing called life by turning chaos to order.

Visual-Spatial: This intelligence refers to the ability to see and comprehend the visual-spatial realm. Broadly, the visual-spatial 'realm' denotes all things that are perceived and conceptualized by your five senses, your sight, hearing and touch especially. People with a high spatial intelligence, intuitively understand the world. They can manipulate objects and things. They know how to build, they know how to organize, and they know how to create physical entities in ways that are precise, innovative, and practical to the world. But visual-spatial people can also understand how the world can be navigated. They might be captains of a ship, or tour guides, or hunters, or pilots. They know how to move themselves and others through natural (and unnatural) surroundings in the most effective, efficient ways. They readily see the smallest details and the biggest pictures; the forest for the trees, and the trees for the forest.

They have a strong sensitivity to colors, lines, shapes, forms and spatial distance. If you or someone you know is high in this intelligence, your best job or career choice is in architecture, art, engineering, city-planning, inventing, landscaping, mapping, photography and/or graphic design. Other careers use this intelligence to a lesser extent.

Bodily-kinesthetic: This is one of these 'intelligences' that many people consider a skill or strength. However, Gardner contends that the ability to manipulate one's body effectively is directly tied to the brain, to the impulses sent from the brain to the body. Moreover, having bodily-kinesthetic intelligence does not mean you are simply a good athlete, skilled in handling a ball or running fast or jumping high, it also means you can make subtle, expressive changes to your physical form.

Consider figure skating or dancing. Consider miming. These individuals are well-coordinated, making all sorts of interpretive, choreographed, and communicative moves and movements in ways most of us can only dream. Balance, coordination, dexterity, strength, pliability, speed, agility and many other factors are all critical to bodily-kinesthetic intelligence. This type of intelligence is not only about using your body to accomplish tasks and reach new heights, it's about transferring feelings, showing emotions, and eliciting emotions from those watching.

But bodily-kinesthetic intelligence is also paired with many others. For instance, visual-spatial intelligence can go hand-in-hand with bodily-kinesthetic. If you use your body well, you likely understand your environment well. You could make a good geologist, or biologist, a good anthropologist, gym teacher, physical therapist, chiropractor or even nurse.

Don't limit yourself when considering your choices. You have a lot of power and that power is critical in determining what you want and where. You. Go.

Musical: This one is pretty self-explanatory. It means you're good at music. We all probably know a person who was always good with instruments. Or always had a tremendous voice. The kid in early primary school who self-taught guitar, who could play the heck outta the drums, or who could listen to a song once or twice and play, sing or rap along with seeming effortlessness.

People with this intelligence are able to not only play and sing music, but detect the most subtle of differences in tone and pitch. They can write music, compose it, discern it critically, perform it, dance to it, and express its emotional quality. Do you or someone you know have a distinct sensitivity to the rhythm, pitch, tone, melody or timbre of music? Can you 'feel' the moods and intentions of a musical piece or score or song? Can you technically analyze the form of music? Can you pick up on the micro-expressions, gestures, and vocal cues involved in musical expression and choreography? Can you direct others how and when to play their instruments or sing in order to create a coherent and moving ensemble?

If so, you might just be *tuned in* to your unique intelligence.

Interpersonal: As previously discussed, this refers to the ability to manage, understand and deal with other people. More than that, it denotes one's capacity to manage other people's thoughts, feelings and emotions. How well do you deal with angry or sad individuals? Can you positively or negatively affect others, seemingly at will? Do you find it hard to relate to others, or is it easy for you to get along with almost anyone? Do you have a lot of friends or are you a loner? Do you choose to be outgoing, or does it come naturally? Do people wear you out or energize you?

When it comes to interpersonal intelligence, what we must remember is that a lot of what we do is natural. The <u>secrets of nonverbal communication</u> are key to this largely *unconscious* process. However, once you make a *conscious* effort to improve these things, they become unconscious. If you are strong in interpersonal intelligence, you simply… 'get' people. You can read their expressions and gestures, you can piece together hidden meanings behind their words and sounds, you understand motivations and intentions, moods and feelings, thoughts and thought patterns. You are sensitive to the small, peculiar, infrequent tics, quirks and cues that others might miss.

Simply put, you're perceptive. And you use that perception to not only influence others, but to understand others, help others, and ultimately help yourself through others.

The best careers and jobs for people high in interpersonal intelligence include: psychologists, psychiatrists, advertisers, counselors, salespersons, therapists, educators, mediators and HR professionals. If you can help others by understanding others, you should never go long without a good, consistent job.

Intrapersonal: Although this particular chapter addresses intrapersonal success, intrapersonal intelligence is slightly different. By having a high intrapersonal intelligence you are likely to have intrapersonal success, but not guaranteed. What this intelligence means is that you understand yourself. In that sense, intrapersonal intelligence is the ability to recognize any and all other intelligences within yourself.

Do you feel that you have an accurate perception of yourself? Do you realistically view your abilities, strengths and weaknesses? Do you know what you can and can't do? Do you take appropriate risks or do you constantly overreach? Are you aware of how you react to different events, settings, and circumstances? Can you predict your moods, motivations and temperaments? Or do you find them hard to control and understand?

How is your self-esteem? Do you struggle with staying motivated and confident? Do you apply self-efficacy principles in a way that is adaptive for everyday life?

Even if your thoughts are negative and your feelings crummy and your behaviors less than ideal, Intrapersonal Intelligence can change this. People high in this intelligence know how to correct bad behaviors. They can step back and examine their own deficiencies with objectivity. They can be honest with themselves about themselves, and are able to distance themselves from things they know to be bad, negative and counterproductive.

The beauty of having a high intrapersonal intelligence is that you can basically do anything with it. If you know how to change your feelings, emotions, thoughts, attitudes and behaviors, then you know how to basically adapt to any situation. Obviously, this is slight exaggeration (we can't simply do anything we put our minds to), but we can do a lot. And what that *lot* means to you, is entirely up to you.

Naturalist: This might seem like a strangely specific intelligence, but if you really think about it, it sort of is its own… 'thing.' People with high naturalist intelligence might be called hippies, and probably like to smoke 'plants' as much as they observe them…

Okay okay, jokes aside… Naturalists have an uncanny ability to, well, recognize nature. They can look at something natural, like clouds or sunlight or mountains or valleys, all sorts of plants, all sorts of animals, even the most minuscule things like a spider there or an ant here—and they can appreciate it. They can understand it. They can recognize, classify and feel connected with it.

However, naturalist intelligence is not restricted to the wide outdoors or the forests or oceans or beaches or deserts. If you grow up in the suburbs or city, you can also have a high naturalist intelligence. This might mean distinguishing between inanimate objects like signs, traffic lights, cars, buildings, roadways, etc. People with this ability may be great with directions, can spot a unique car out of hundreds, and can make sudden, correct decisions while exploring an environment for the first time.

People high in this intelligence will undoubtedly be good at pattern recognition. They may make good analysts, good scouts, good tour guides, good biologists or urban planners or conservationists or wildlife experts. They can be scientists that study all sorts of animals and plants. They can be filmmakers that document the natural world. They can be engineers that understand how to layout a city or community. The job opportunities for a naturalist are actually way more eclectic than one might think. If you're high in this intelligence, consider yourself lucky. And do, whatever you do, naturally.

Existential (Metaphysical): This final type of intelligence deals with the bigger issues, the deeper thoughts, the more pressing humanitarian concerns. Think a philosopher. Think an absent-minded professor. Think a spacey dreamer. Think a writer focused on social commentary, on understanding the broad, sweeping problems of the world. Or a journalist. Or a producer or director of an indie art film. Or a shaman. Or a spiritual guru.

Whatever the job or manifestation of existential intelligence, it is almost undoubtedly 'big picture.' These individuals may not be good at the day-to-day stuff, or at focusing on menial details, but they certainly know how to think outside the box. They'll ponder the meaning of life, the fate of our planet, the future of mankind, the reason for dying—the deep, philosophical, probing thoughts that most people try not to consider.

If you're metaphysical or existential, you might find 'normal' jobs a little tough. Too unsatisfying. Too predictable. Too boring or formulaic.

The good news is, you're probably quite smart. You might not be a fast test-taker, or the first to answer a question, but that's only because you're seeing all the angles. Sometimes to a fault. You have a tendency to overanalyze, to think deeply not quickly, to withhold judgment until you've considered every possibility.

No matter what you do with this intelligence, rest assured. Your ideas have value, great value, it might just take some time to find a buyer.

Okay, so that's it.

We've covered all nine intelligences in Gardner's Multiple Intelligence Theory. Truth is, every one of us has a bit of each. Some of us are lucky to be high in one or many, some of us may be mediocre in most, or even very low in some. And some of us, are total savants, idiots in many areas, but absolutely, undeniably, off-the-charts in one area. Ever met somebody who is a genius in one respect, but can barely hold a conversation, or tie a shoe, or make a sandwich, yet can do advanced Calculus in their head, or write an incredible 20-pg paper in a matter of hours? Or somebody who can barely read or write but can rebuild a car from scratch?

Ever met somebody who doesn't seem particularly amazing at anything, but you know when you need help in an area of weakness, they'll at least be able to help? Ever met somebody who seems to know everything about everything? Every met somebody who seems totally clueless, no matter what you're talking about, yet somehow he or she can zip through a test like it's nothing? As if he or she is intentionally *hiding* intelligence to fit in?

Ever met somebody who, well, just seems really, really… dumb?

You get the picture. We're all different. We all have unique abilities, and sometimes they're hard to pinpoint. And this is why Gardner's theory is so important, and applied in so many domains, from education to business to counseling to even job applications. The IQ score, in many people's minds, is too limiting. After all, can you—everything that makes you, *you*—be reduced to a single score? Is the sum of your parts totally captured by a single number? Does a standardized test score encapsulate *you*?

Of course not, and that's why knowing where you are smart, and not so smart, is so so critical.

Your ability is your gateway. It is your lease on a new life. It is your springboard for distant targets, your pathway to a new place. But only if you let it be. Only if you, and every faculty within you, make it so.

Because what is intelligence, what is ability, what is all the talent in the world… without *Motivation*?

The Motivation Driver

Motivation is a funky thang. One minute you're about to workout, work, rest, work some more, hang with family, meet some friends, and cram a million and one different things into fewer hours than you can count on one hand – and then you're *done*.

DONE.

Saying *'screw it'* with your plans gone out the window. Doing nothing, kicking back on the couch with a good snack and a guilty conscience.

Motivation. That's what they call it, some have it in bundles, some seemingly never. It's what keeps some of us going and going, while others are asleep at the wheel. Motivation. The main difference between those who *have it* but don't use it, and those who *use it* and get ahead.

Sometimes you wanna do so much you never do a thing. Other times you suddenly have a knack, you do a little, you do a little, and before you know it you've done a lot. Sometimes, we plan it out and get it done. And some days, well… we can barely be bothered to leave our beds.

Motivation is what separates the winners from the losers. You've probably heard it. It's what turns potential into productivity, it's what gets results when the other, smarter, better, superior guy/gal is sitting back and slacking off.

Motivation is a character trait and personal strength. Or, it's the weakest link in the whole darn chain.

We've all been there. We just can't seem to… 'get in the mood.' We don't want to, we don't 'feel it,' we make excuses, and grab coffee, and eat more food, and surf the web, and chat with friends, and move around all restless and annoyed—anything, *anything* to keep from doing the one thing we need to do.

Sometimes we actually *want to* do it. Or so we think. But we just.. can't.. seem.. to get it going. We feel bad. We feel weird. We feel totally incapable.

And then it happens…

A day we can't actually believe. Where everything clicks, and our brain is on fire and our thoughts are seamless, our feelings steady, every faculty attuned and ready. We get sh*t done and we get it done fast, and we aren't rushing, but flowing, not forcing but working, engaged and moving and interconnected with the balance of the universe.

Or something…

Point is, we are all capable of optimizing motivation. All it takes is a little perspective. And that perspective all starts with a little understanding of the Attributional Theory.

The Attributional Theory has been around for a while now, and is considered a presiding concept in theories of motivation and social psychology. One central tenet in this theory, as it relates to human motivational is *Intrapersonal* Attribution.

Consider an event, any event. It can be something as minor as spilling a glass of water, to something as big as getting in a major car accident, losing a job, or losing a spouse or loved one to death or rejection. Now consider the outcome.

Say you spilled a glass of water. What happens? Did it get all over the floor? Did it spill something valuable? Did the glass break in the process? Or how about that car accident? What is the outcome? Are you hurt? Are you spared? Is somebody else in the car or in another car seriously injured? Or how about the losing of a job, or the losing of a spouse or loved one due to death or rejection? What is the outcome? Are you out on the street? Are you all alone? Are you finally free from a toxic relationship? Are things more or less the same, or does everything feel like it's changed?

Once you have discerned the outcome, think of that outcome differently. It is not only an outcome, but it's also a stimulus. It's a stimulus because it 'stimulates' a response, a certain, definable behavioral response.

So what's your response?

In the event of the water spilling… Do you curse in anger? Do you laugh at your clumsiness? Do you feel thankful that it 'was only water' or that it didn't get on something nearby? How about following the stimulus in the accident? Depending upon who was or wasn't hurt, do you thank your lucky stars it wasn't worse? Do you have a breakdown? Are you more worried about the costs of repairs and insurance hike? If you're not paying the car bill, are you worried how the person who is will react? Were you drunk or high? Are you scared, or are you too… 'gone' to care?

If you lose your spouse or loved one to death or rejection, what's the reaction? Are you incredibly angry? Depressed?

What are the ending behavioral reactions? In the case of the car accident, do you stop driving for a while? In the case of spilling water, do you drink from only bottles or only in certain areas of your residence? In the case of losing a loved one or family member, do you withdraw? Do you go to counseling? What are the end behavioral reactions? What steps do you take?

Now STOP.

We skipped a step. In between those behavioral reactions just mentioned and the stimulus, there is what we call the attribution. The attribution refers to where we place the cause. To what or to whom do we assign fault or responsibility.

Now, when things are int*ra*personal, we assign fault in ourselves. When things are int*er*personal, we assign fault outside ourselves.

So think upon the previous scenarios. Your behavioral reaction will depend directly on your attributions. In fact, you will endure both psychological and behavioral consequences as a result. If you blame yourself for being clumsy for spilling the water, your behavioral reaction will be self-directed. You might feel stupid or get angry. However, if you blame your immediate environment for being responsible (too much clutter, you slipped, etc.), then you will not attribute the cause to yourself.

In the case of the car accidents and losing of loved ones, again, intrapersonal attribution will put the blame squarely on you, and inside you. Maybe when you got in the car accident you were distracted, playing with the radio, listening to music, listening to someone else. Maybe you were speeding, or not looking.

If you make an *inter*personal attribution, then you'll likely blame those outside you. The accident happened because of the weather, or the other person driving, or because there was simply nothing you could do and it was a rare, bad incident.

Similarly, in the cases of losing a loved one due to death or rejection… it all comes down to attribution. Your resulting emotions will depend on the attribution. If you attribute the death of a loved one to uncontrollable factors (*he was old, the medical event was unforeseen, there was nothing we could do*) then you'll probably still feel terrible and sad… but you won't feel guilty.

Now, what if you attribute that death to yourself? What if you feel shameful or guilty for not helping your old aunt, for never getting her that new medication, for not checking in enough to make sure everything was okay? Do you feel you bear some brunt of the responsibility? Do you feel bad like you could have prevented it?

In the case of losing a spouse or being shunned by a family member, where do you attribute the responsibility? Do you blame that spouse or family member for being impossible to live with or deal with? Did your wife or husband cheat on you? Did your brother or sister or father or mother mistreat you? Was he or she abusive? Mean-spirited? Unloving?

Or do you assign the blame intrapersonally? Do you feel like you were the one doing things wrong? Did you drive them away? Did you give them no choice? Should you have changed your lifestyles but you refused, or couldn't, or didn't know how—and now you're all alone?

Now consider motivation more broadly. In all these scenarios, what happens now? What do you do moving forward?

What matters at this point are two things, what Attributional Theory terms: expectancy and value. Generally, expectancy refers to one's subjective feelings about future outcomes—successful or not—and value refers to the emotional magnitude of those successes or failures.

Expectancy depends primarily on the perceived stability or instability of factors. For instance, if you believe that getting in a car accident is due to a stable cause, such as your poor driving, your lack of awareness, or generally other bad drivers on the road, you might expect that another accident is simply unavoidable. However, if you believe that the cause of you getting in an accident is unstable, your expectations change. In this case, you feel that it depends on your mood, the day, if you choose to be more observant, if road conditions are different, etc.

The same applies to losing a relationship. You might find that this is caused by stable factors, that you or others are simply incompatible, that you're not a 'people person,' that you are not good at relationships no matter what you do, or that other people simply don't 'get' you. Or, you might find the cause unstable, believing that it can and does change, and that you might be able to avoid another rejection or loss through said change.

Again, it depends on where you attribute these factors. Locus and control refer to this. Locus is where you place the cause, in yourself or outside yourself, and control is whether you feel something can be controlled or not. But be warned, even if you think the locus is inside you, that doesn't mean you can control it. You might have been born un-athletic, so the locus is you, but the control is outside of you (ie; you don't get sports scholarships, you don't get awards for your participation, you don't get picked for the varsity squad, etc.).

In the end, it's all about how you think about yourself and your surroundings. Do you think that you have something that is stable and outside of your control? Do you blame your problems on things you can't change, thus resulting in feelings of insecurity, shame, guilt, inability and sadness?

There are many ways to consider events. There are many ways to impact motivation. Take one scenario. Let's say you were in school and you failed a test. Now, where do you attribute responsibility? Do you consider yourself dumb or stupid at one subject, and thus things will never change? Or, because you attribute the cause to yourself, do you believe you can change? Do you believe by studying smarter, working harder, and trying new strategies, you can overcome?

Now what if you fail the test and then you immediately attribute the responsibility outside yourself? Maybe you blame the teacher for not understanding your learning style, for not liking you, for being unnecessarily hard on you and downgrading you while going easy on others? The question is, do you consider this controllable or not? If you attribute blame to your teacher, are you essentially saying things won't change? Or do you believe that you can alter that relationship, persuade your teacher, appease your teacher, or bring your teacher to an understanding that favors your test performances moving forward?

Again, there are many ways to think of motivation. To stay motivated or lose it all. To push beyond your self-perceived barriers, or fall weak and give in.

Who are you? What do you do? And how do you keep doing it?

Motivation, in its many forms and functions, is the answer to that question...

The Thought-Behavior Dyad

Sometimes, however, motivation isn't enough.

You aren't working hard enough. You just don't have it. You try but you falter. You don't just fail, you fail to start. You fail to care. You fail to get your butt off the ground and get going when the time is ripe, and the opportunities are boundless.

Simply put, you're a bum.

And you don't know why. You wish you knew, you wish you could just be motivated, all the time, like that *other* person, but you aren't.

So why?

What is your reason, not just your excuse, not just your momentary or temporary line of b.s. – what is your *reason*? Think deeply. What is the underlying reason, or cause, of your lack of motivation. Of your, shall we say, *amotivational syndrome*?

Why can't you simply work as consistently, and intelligently, as you desire?

Why can't you? What, in the world, is your problem?

If you, like millions of people, cannot possibly answer these questions clearly—then stop. Take a breath and look closely, and stop.

It is time... for CBT...

In case you have never heard of it, Cognitive-Behavioral Therapy (CBT) is a type of therapy, intervention and treatment that addresses your problems based on two things: your cognitions (thoughts) and your behaviors. Your mental problems, your emotional issues, and your psychological disorders are all related directly to your thoughts and the behaviors that stem from them.

It's a feedback loop. You think a certain way, you act a certain way, and then as a consequence of those behaviors, you continue to think that certain way, thus continuing those behaviors. Take, for instance, a drug addict. They might think, *'I'm worthless.'* So they abuse drugs, because, hey, what difference does it make? They've already concluded they'll never amount to anything or contribute to the world, so might as well waste their days getting high and feeling artificially good.

Then what happens? The original thought of worthlessness/hopelessness contributes to drugging behaviors, which then… lead to more worthless/hopeless behaviors.

If you lose your job, wake up late, have no money, have no relationships, and your only friend is the guy down the hall with the spoon and the rock, chances are you're going to feel like crap all the time. Thus, your thoughts will be dark and crappy, and you'll view your weak, sickly state as worthless.

And if you're worthless and hopeless, whaddaya do?

More drugs!

But that's an extreme example, and we're getting off track…

Bottom line is this: we all have cognitions (or thoughts), and some are adaptive and some are maladaptive. When it comes to cognitions, the bad ones lead to emotional distress and bad behaviors, the good ones lead to good emotions and behaviors. Simple enough?

Well, your cognitions are also tied to your sense of self, your sense of history (past/present/future) and your sense of the world. This last one, sense of the world is called schemata.

Schemata is a psychological term which refers to your structuring of perceptions. How you view all the constant stimuli your brain processes.

Let's take one scenario to demonstrate how adaptive and maladaptive cognitions can differ:

(1) Your boss at work asks you to do something extra.

Okay, so you're at work, maybe you love it, maybe you hate it, maybe you're somewhere in the middle. Whatever the case, you just found out that you now have to do some extra work. Now, there are a million ways you could react to this news, but let's view it from two extremes: maladaptive and adaptive.

First, the adaptive. So you hear this and you immediately think to yourself, *'Oh okay, I can do that. That's not bad.'* After some greater reflection you conclude, *'this is actually good. I'll be able to prove myself in outside tasks, maybe garner some greater attention and position myself for that eventual raise/promotion I've been seeking.'* Although you feel the stress of this new task, you think, *'that's okay, stress is good if I use it.'*

So you use it. And you plan ahead, and you work hard, and intelligently, and you get your work and this new work done. In the end, perhaps, your results are good and your boss takes notice. In the long-term, you benefit.

Now, consider the maladaptive cognitions.

You struggle. You hear that your boss wants you to do extra work, and your first thought is, *'Freakin great.'* You tell yourself, *'Like he'll care if I do a good job'* and now you're even more mad, because *'Others get to slack but here I am getting extra work? B.S.'*

So what happens?

You don't see it as an opportunity, but a hindrance, a hassle. You don't work hard on it, you perform poorly, your interactions with your boss and coworkers are negative, and a potential chance of gaining more credence in your company is wasted.

Now, sometimes you are right to be 'negative' in your thoughts.

In fact, negative thoughts do not necessarily mean they are maladaptive. If a drugged-out criminal has a gun to your head and asks for your money, thinking too positively could get you killed. If you have a… 'rosy' perspective and think, *'I'll just tell him he's a nice person,'* you might get shot. However, if you think negatively, *'crap I gotta give him my money or he could kill me,'* you're probably right. In this case, having a dark, but rational, perspective is the adaptive cognition, and thinking extremely optimistically is unrealistic and maladaptive.

It all depends on the situation you're in. It might be good to be slightly negative about a new diagnosis if that means you'll be more likely to take your medication. If being too positive - *'I'll overcome severe diabetes through positive thoughts alone'* - is leading to disastrous results, then it's maladaptive.

But sometimes it's not easy. Sometimes, you have to test your cognitions. Really look at them, and understand why you feel and behave that way. There are two important ways to do this:

(1) *Challenge the validity.* In other words, a validity test. Are your thoughts valid? That is to say, do they address what they're supposed to address? More specifically, do your thoughts address what they intend to address realistically?

Take for instance, the case of getting in a traffic jam on your way to work. You're mad. You're more than mad. Your thought is: *'F this S*it, now I'm gonna be late, and so-and-so will be down my neck, Hell I could get f*ckin fired for this sh*t, this stupid f*ckin piece of s'*—Okay.

Does that sound like a reasonable response? Do those seem like practical thoughts? Are your thoughts valid? That is to say, are they adequately addressing the situation, with the correct scope and scale? Are you stuck in a traffic jam or the jaws of a great white shark??

Clearly, the above reaction is overblown. Now, that doesn't mean there weren't reasons for it. Maybe you didn't sleep well, ran outta coffee that morning, had to run out the door since you were already late, have so much to do, it's hot outside, people are driving strangely for some reason, and— so yea, it's a total mess and your thoughts reflect that. You're pissed, you're pessimistic, and you think the whole world is conspiring against you.

Now... let's take another person in the same situation with more valid cognitions.

There's a traffic jam, but instead of ranting and raving, this individual takes a breath. He or she recognizes that these things happen. You can always call ahead and let your boss know. You're a little tired from lack of sleep, you wish you had coffee, but there are worse problems in the world. You don't like being late, but what can you do? You check your GPS for traffic patterns, turn up your favorite radio station and ride it out.

(2) *Challenge the Reliability.* If validity represents how accurately your thoughts address an event, reliability represents how *frequently* your thoughts are valid.

Take the previous scenario. Okay, so you got in a traffic jam. Now, ask yourself this. How often do you get in traffic jams? Maybe getting mad, or thinking it's a big deal is actually more adaptive than maladaptive. Why? Well, let's say every time you've gotten in traffic jams on your particular route, they're bad. Not minor ones, but long, drawn-out ones that can add an hour or more to your trek. So then what? Well, getting angry might actually be adaptive, because you are reliably understanding what this jam represents. Getting angry and making a big deal out of it might cause a behavioral change (ie; you choose a route less likely to have jams, you start leaving earlier, you search for a different job, etc.).

If yours cognitions are *un*reliable, you might think of a traffic jam (that is always long) as not a big deal. You might inaccurately think, *'it'll be short and sweet'* even though every time before it has been the opposite of short and sweet. As a result, you might never change your driving habits, and frequently end up late to work, leading to problems with your employer, negative feedback, poor job performance, etc.

If your cognitions are valid, they accurately represent the situation. They are proportional to what is going on and contribute to adaptive feelings and behaviors. If your cognitions are reliable, they demonstrate repeated validity, leading to repeated adaptive feelings and behaviors...

A famous person once said, *'Trying the same thing and expecting different results is the definition of insanity.'*

Are you crazy or not?

Now, cognitive behavioral therapy (CBT) is more than just thinking rationally and adaptively. It's more than just having positive or negative thoughts, or considering yourself right or wrong, bad or good, in your feelings and behaviors.

CBT is a very real, very researched, very well-understood class of therapies <u>for all sorts of problems</u>.

Let's take a look:

For *issues with addiction*:

CBT is considered mildly effective for all sorts of drug and substance abuse disorders and problems. However, CBT is considered especially effective for cannabis and nicotine abuse, but not as strong for <u>treating addiction to alcohol</u> and opiates. The reason these effects range is dependent upon the drug and type of abuse. Some people might binge drink, others might drink every day. Some people might depend on chain-smoking when stressed, others might smoke a little, but every single day without stop. Some people abuse drugs and alcohol due to unrelated past problems or insecurity issues. Other people abuse drugs and alcohol during phases, relating to stressors such as work, family, and mourning. Understanding these nuances is critical to analyzing why some people have cognitions that gear them toward abusing drugs and alcohol.

For *depression and sadness*:

Although research indicates that CBT can help us understand why we feel sad, with feelings of guilt, hopelessness, shame, loneliness and the like, CBT alone is not nearly as effective as when paired with medication.

That said, CBT may be effective for depressed individuals because it forces us to look into the source of our sadness. Are we permanently 'down' or are we just going through a period of 'the blues' ? Many of the reasons we feel hopeless are due to lifestyle. We don't sleep well, we don't have healthy relationships, we don't exercise enough or eat well enough. In fact, a healthy, clear and clean conscience is directly related to clean eating, and what some experts have termed <u>neurogenic dieting.</u>

When we think of our depression, consider this: why do we beat up on ourselves? Why do we feel like nothing matters? When we view something, anything, as simple as a conversation with someone, or a person's attitude, do we feel good or bad? Do we doubt ourselves due to past failures? Do we think its innate or do we believe we can change our environment and our outcomes? Do we have trouble getting going because our family members never encouraged us? Did we have a poor childhood? Abuse, neglect, lack of positive reinforcement? Are we the <u>adult children of alcoholics</u>? Is there a history of depression or drug abuse in our family?

Considering these problems is just the start to using CBT and seeking counsel.

For *eating disorders*:

Compared to other forms of psychotherapy, CBT is significantly more effective and powerful for treating bulimia and anorexia in particular. The reasons for this are not entirely known, but research suggests that people with these disorders believe they are fat based on false comparisons and poor self-image. By changing the way they think, and perceive, they are able to modulate the way they behave. Instead, they are taught to treat food as nourishment, not danger. They change their thoughts in order to reward themselves for healthy lifestyles, to improve their bodies and minds through clean and safe eating programs. People with eating disorders who view starvation or excess eating as stress responses must learn to reconceptualize their stress management techniques. As many have learned through CBT, stress is not necessarily bad or good, but a <u>critical</u>

<u>evolutionary force</u> optimized for overall health and well-being.

For *personality disorders*:

In case you haven't heard of them, personality disorders are maladaptive clusters of traits that create problematic personalities. These include borderline personality, narcissistic personality, antisocial personality, and a number of others. CBT has been found to have large efficacy for individuals with these disorders, especially in cases of anger and hostility. Understanding why you act the way you do, is often linked directly to your thoughts and feelings.

Typically, people with antisocial disorder will hate all things establishment. They may have a history of bad relations with people, places and things and may harbor deep-seated feelings that simply do not go away without serious reflection and adjustment. CBT serves as a catalyst for these feelings, and many others, in order to also address related thoughts and behaviors. Similarly, people with narcissistic personality may view themselves as superior, often putting others down in mean-spirited, unsustainable ways. CBT highlights the reasons for these thoughts and behaviors, often linked to compensation for low self-esteem.

For *stress management*:

When it comes to life, we all know stress. Things never go as smoothly as we wish, and life never seems to give us what we want at the exact moment, or in the exact way, we expect. If you can learn stress, manage stress, and even use stress for positive results, then you can succeed. CBT addresses these efforts by teaching us how to think, and react to, the most basic and the most advanced stressors. Everything from struggling with life's little moments, to devising coping mechanisms for huge problems, such as illness, death, and other irreparable life changes.

For *children and elders*:

Many children struggle with self-esteem and insecurity. Given today's social media age, children more than ever are subjected to all forms of peer comparisons and external pressures, such as cyber bullying and shaming. By changing social media use, perceptions, and comprehensions, CBT teaches children to understand why they feel, think and act the way they do. With all the sheer 'noise' out there distracting our kids today, it's no wonder some might need a little extra guidance. Fortunately, CBT is there to help.

Elders also need CBT. Older men and women experience certain issues as they age. Aside from the obvious physical deterioration, these adults may have trouble remembering, difficulty concentrating and thinking, and problems with everyday tasks. As a result, they become frustrated. They grow tired. They grow angry. They misplace blame. They project onto others. They become depressed, despondent, and may even begin to consider death or suicide. They grow lonely as their families send them to retirement homes and assisted living facilities. By and large, many elderly people have a lot to overcome.

CBT helps by restructuring their cognitions. They learn to use words such as "can" and "will" as opposed to "can't" and "won't" – although small, these words present significant changes. This cognitive-textual framing is incredibly useful for removing limiting beliefs and adding expanding beliefs.

Elders also learn to think more positively generally, and to contemplate their problems through new ways. Pro-social interests, humorous thoughts, and realistic appraisals are all part of using CBT toward efficacious ends.

Clearly, CBT has its many uses. It can be combined with other therapies, used as a standalone, and incorporated as part of a multi-modal medication/therapy/lifestyle change. It can be part of a holistic regimen or its own unique treatment. No matter what you do, CBT is powerful, it is undeniable, and it can change your life for the better.

So don't delay. Read up on CBT and apply it today. Either learn to do it on your own or seek professional treatment. Apply the techniques and optimize the strategies. You never know just how well things could go…

But wait. CBT itself isn't the solution. Remember, CBT is for *you*. It is a class of treatments, strategies and interventions focused on *you*. But what if you don't wanna focus on you? What if *you*, want to focus on others?

What if instead of int*ra*personal treatment, you need int*er*personal treatment? What if you want to change the way others feel, think and behave? What if you've concluded that the problem isn't you, but those *around* you? Those affecting you? Those who control many of the external factors inside and outside the world nearby you? Then what?

Well...

Interpersonal Success: The Top Power Multipliers

If you want to fully maximize success, you need to look out. You need to think deep and go deeper. But most importantly, you must learn to seek the outer realm, when the inner one leaves you lacking.

Some of us, simply need to learn body language.

Body language is one of those things that continuously mystifies. Even when you think you have it figured out, you get thrown a curve ball. Something happens, an expression means something different, a gesture is mysterious, a voice tone changes, words and meanings separate and interweave and all of it seems one thing when suddenly it's another.

One day you think you can read the random dude on the street. The next day you can't even understand your lifelong friend. It happens. And one reason it happens is because body language comes in clusters.

Clusters. Not one sign. Not one move or movement or pose or smile—but all of them, taken together, mixed holistically, leading to one communication over the others.

But even clusters can be deceiving. And if you're dealing with an especially perplexing person, a master of deception or a genius of the body, body language is a conundrum all its own.

So break the code. If you're dealing with people, or a person, you can't understand, you can't decipher—it's time to stop. Take a breath and see the world for what it is. Become a master of body language yourself. Learn the one simple equation to quantify it all...

Quantifying Body Language for Ultimate Interpersonal Success

The first three things you need to know when it comes to becoming a master of body language are this: breathe, move, talk. This is how you connect. I repeat. Breathe. Move. Talk.

If you can do this, you can start simply and keep going.

But you have to do these three things. They are the three quantities you need to embrace. It honestly doesn't matter what the body language means. If you want a primer on body language, there are plenty of those. But if you want interpersonal success, through body language, all you have to do is mirror.

Model and mirror to connect. Remember, imitation is the highest form of flattery. Birds of a feather flock together. Look the same, act the same. Breathe. Move. Talk. Connect. B + M + T = C

Let's go through quantities of the equation:

(B) Breathe:

Breathing is important because it is an unconscious process. But also, it keeps us alive. When we stop, we die. When we breathe faster, we're worked up. Either through emotions, exercise, or some other stimulant like drugs. When we breathe slower, we're calm, collected, resting, or perhaps under the influence of substances like sedatives.

By breathing like somebody else, you are essentially saying: *I get you.*

But you are saying it without saying it. Breathing is far less noticeable than other things. Somebody might know if you're matching them if you cross your legs when they cross their legs; or stand the way they stand, or make a similar expression to theirs.

But breathing… breathing is subtle. Chances are they won't notice how you're breathing. But you have to notice them. So look, look closely, at their chest, their diaphragm, and their mouth. Slowly, but surely, change your breathing. If they're gasping after exercise or something else, give them a second to calm down, then match your rate with theirs. Sometimes it's as easy as listening. Some people are simply heavy breathers, even at rest. Other times you might have to use environmental cues, like the rustling of their shirt, or their exhales in the cold air. Whatever it is you're doing, do it subtly, and do it steadily. No need to suddenly start breathing like them—that might look fake.

Instead, be steady and be sure. And be careful, you don't get found out!

(M) Move:

This means movement. You have to, have to, have to match the other person's movements. This one is a little harder. But the best way to do it is to do it slowly. Don't mimic the first move. Examine the person for at least a few minutes, nodding and talking as naturally as possible. Get a feel for his or her regular movements.

We all have tendencies. Some people will scratch their eye or rub their hair. Some people tilt their chin or rub their neck. Some people have nervous tics where they look over somewhere real quick, twitch their nose or move their shoulders. A lot of people just scratch, bob, jerk and move about in funny ways, oftentimes not even realizing it.

But they will realize it. Unconsciously. If you do it.

And that's where this matters. If you do it unconsciously like they do it unconsciously, their brain registers something. It recognizes something similar in you, and even if the two of you are in a heated dispute, some part of that other person feels inextricably connected to you.

However small, some part of them will feel a connection, and then that's when you can control them…

Masters of body language will be able to adopt another person's mannerisms and movements, and then hijack them. Before you know it, they're following you. One moment they scratch their face every 30 seconds as part of a nervous tic… then 2 minutes later you've got them scratching their nose and chin every *15* seconds, without even realizing it, because you've *hijacked* the tic.

Sound too crazy to be true?

Believe it. And the best part of it all? If you do it well, if you do mirror them seamlessly and believably—which takes a lot of practice—they'll like you even more ;)

But at the end of the day, the key is not to hijack. You can if you want, but most times our goal is simply to connect, to establish a rapport. And if that's your goal, to make them like you for an increased chance of success—then mimicking movement is the way to get it.

(T) Talk:

This might seem counter intuitive to *body* language, but actually it's quite important. By talk, I do not mean actual words. Well, not exactly. What I'm suggesting is the use of words, the mimicking of words, the style of words, the order and choice of words.

The trick is to reflect it right back on them, so that you are talking the way they talk, with a similar inflection, tone and meaning. Let's say one person uses power words a lot. They say "will" and "do" and "can" and "win" and "make" and "achieve" a lot. Or maybe somebody else is tentative in speech, saying "like" and "sorta" and "kinda" and "ya know" frequently. Maybe somebody speaks in quick utterances then somewhat stutters, or takes long pauses or breaths… or maybe somebody else seems long-winded, talking slowly and meandering about, moving from topic to topic.

It might take you a while to notice these idiosyncrasies. But over time you will. Some people are straight talkers, others are avoidant, hiding their true thoughts and feelings by using words vaguely, or extremely carefully. Some people are guarded, some people are open. Some people have Freudian slips and say what they mean to say, only to quickly correct themselves.

Also look for sensory language. People who use visual language tend to be stronger in visual-spatial intelligence. They might say things like, "I see" or "I picture" or "it looks like" or "I imagine" and so on. Other people might be more auditory-based. They'll say things like, "sounds like" or "I hear" "word is" or "it's been said," and so on. Other people are more tactile-based in their speech. They say things like "I feel" and "I get the sense" or "I sense" or "I get the feeling."

Overall, all of these word choices come together with the person's tone of voice, speech patterns, movements and breathing, to form the critical three quantities of the 'Connection' equation.

When you have pieced all of these separate, but related, parts together—then you're onto something. Then you're beginning to understand how to truly connect with another person. It doesn't even matter if you know what's being communicated. Remember, establishing a rapport or connection is about mirroring. It's about the unconscious similarities in B, M & T that bind us. If you can mimic, you can match. And if you want to do more than match, to go above and beyond, and dominate, then you can do that too...

Reconceptualizing the Body Language Ratio

Now let's reconsider some previous concepts.

Tone of voice. Body language. And words.

We all understand tone of voice. When your mom or dad yelled at you as a youngster, they used a stern, lower tone of voice. When they were happy with you, they spoke softer or more sweetly. It didn't matter what words they used, you got the sense they were happy or unhappy, based on the way they expressed those words.

Just think of a dog. If you've messed with a dog, you've probably noticed… You can say *anything* you want if you say it the right way. You can tell a dog it's a dumb big lump of lard, but if you say it in a high-pitched tone, the dog's tail will wag, its tongue will dangle, and it will be happy. If however, you say something extremely nice, *'you're the best dog in the world, Wolfy'* but say it in a deep, loud reprimanding tone, your dog will act like it just got slapped.

Now onto Body Language. For the sake of clarity, let's define body language as all things strictly related to your body. So that will include all things you consciously and unconsciously do, physically. This can be expressions, gestures, moves, movements, tics, postures, positions, involuntary spasms, sensations, you name it. Anything pertaining strictly to your body, not spoken, and not having to do with any noise relating to spoken words.

Now onto Words. By words, we are talking strictly about, well, words. Not the sound of words, just the words. Not any noise associated with the words, but the words themselves. This distinction can be a little vague, so think of it this way: imagine that the spoken words are written. Remove any sort of intonation or inflection and just look at the words. This incorporates the word choice, the order of words, the frequency of certain words, the definition of words.

Now, obviously this is a simplistic breakdown.

As you can imagine, all of these three things are connected and interwoven. After all, the meaning of a word might depend upon how it is conveyed or stated. Is it formal or slang? Is it said quickly or drawn-out? Emphasized or de-emphasized? Said softly or loudly? And what does the person do when saying it? Do they move one way or another? Do they look away or roll their eyes and scratch their head or hide their face?

Okay, so we all agree, it's abundantly clear: words, tone and body language are inseparable… right? They can't simply be separated and considered distinct entities… right?

Wrong. Well, sorta wrong, depending on, uh, well, who you ask. See…

There's this little thing called the Mehrabian Rule, also known as the 7-38-55 Rule. According to this long-lasting rule, the words, tone of voice, and body language of a given person each account for 7%, 38%, and 55% of interpersonal communication. Albert Mehrabian, the man and UCLA professor behind this long-lasting rule, created this 'rule' in the 1960s.

But many disagree.

You can't quantify it, they say. You can't ever possibly separate these things, say others. You can do nothing and think nothing and know nothing but what you know from already having known you didn't know you knew…

- what?

Symbiotic Theory

Okay, so if you're confused by now, it's because you overthought it.

Fact is, the Mehrabian rule may be nice in theory, to say and hear in business conferences, and psychological classrooms, but in reality – it's hard to say. It's hard to break down the effect of these three separate things, because it depends on a number of things: namely, how you define 'body language' 'tone of voice' and 'words,' who is demonstrating and perceiving them, why they are being demonstrated and perceived, when they are being demonstrated and perceived, where they are being demonstrated and perceived, and in what what they are being demonstrated and perceived.

Your body language might say something completely different depending upon the situation.

If you say, 'I'm great' and you look pale and are jittery, you probably communicate that you're not great.

If you say, 'I'm great' and you look youthful with light in your eyes, you probably communicate that you are great.

Now, the tone of voice, words and body language might be slightly different in both of these extremes. There are nuances, maybe there are some looks or quick movements, maybe even subtle changes in voice that you don't consciously register, or slight hesitations in the words, or the pronunciation, or even tiny, tiny accents.

It also depends, as previously said, who is saying and perceiving the tone of voice, words and body language. If somebody says *I'm great*, that might mean something different depending upon the person who says it. Maybe the person saying it means he or she is a tremendous person, and not necessarily feeling well or good at the time. Maybe the person who hears it thinks it means the person saying it is strong or powerful.

Cultural and sub-cultural and societal and linguistic differences also exist. Saying you are good will mean something entirely different. Some harmless words in one culture are highly offensive or taboo in another. Some words simply don't have a counterpart or meaning in one culture vs. another.

What all this says, is simple: It's tough to say, just how much of a *percentage* tone of voice, words and body language account for the average person's interpretation.

So let's get away from the 7-38-55 Rule. Let's enter into what I term, the Symbiotic Theory.

The Symbiotic Theory:

This theory basically presupposes that people communicate in different ways, and that these ways and their effects are all interrelated.

Now, do not be mistaken. This Theory doesn't necessarily say that an effect is positive. For instance, you might choose to communicate in a way that is confusing or deceptive. Perhaps you'll say one thing, but display body language that contradicts what you said. *"I'd love to help,"* you might say, as you look annoyed and in a hurry. Sometimes we do these things consciously, many times unconsciously. But these things always, always work together toward a given effect.

Now, if you don't realize it, there are many reasons why people do things for… 'effect.'

Oftentimes we just want to get along. But some of us, of course, want to create friction. We want to dominate. We want to win. We want to move people at our whim, like pawns on a chessboard. At the end of the day, we want to be able to consciously use our body language to enhance our lives in ways we see fit. Sometimes, these behaviors fail. Sometimes they backfire. And sometimes, just sometimes, they work so well, so effortlessly, that we feel like we can read others' minds…

The Symbiotic Theory accounts for all of this.

Think of the following situation: the dating world. <u>Covert sexual body language</u> is something every single man or woman wants to know. But it can only be achieved in one way. By creating intrigue. You can't win a woman or man by being easy and predictable. You can't seduce a man or woman by being boring, by not having that 'it' factor. Let any pick up artist or dating guru tell you, attraction is created. It is magnetism. It is power. It is mystery. It is confidence. But most importantly, it is combination.

You have to combine your tone of voice, your words and your body language. Think of it this way. If you want to pick up that sexy someone, you have to catch them off guard. Your body language can't say, *'I'm so horny omg omg you're so sexy please let me have you'*—No

And your body language also shouldn't say that you're not interested in the slightest.

There needs to pull and push. Likewise, your tone of voice and words must have some pull and push. You have to keep them guessing. Say something that grabs his or her interest, but show some disinterest with your body language. At times, indicate interest with your tone of voice, then lack of attraction, then obvious attraction, then maybe none at all. Play your three main tools off one another. In other words, use your tone of voice, words and body language to get what you want. Make the person second-guess if you want them. Make them chase *you*. If you're a risk-taker, go for with it. Say things that would normally indicate clear disinterest, but show extreme intense interest with your body language. Use dichotomous actions to keep that special man or woman, guy or gal wondering – and working – to figure you out.

It's the best way and the best method. Never be obvious, never go all in. Remember, it is called Symbiotic for a reason. You want these qualities to interact to get the desired effect. You want them to be mutually beneficial.

Some call this intermittent reinforcement.

Think of a pet. If you give your pet a treat every time it does a certain something, your pet will learn to expect that something. It will beg for and demand that something. However, if you don't always give that something, your pet won't be sure. Furthermore, if you give your pet that something in an endlessly predictable way, your pet might get bored. It'll get bored because it knows it can get it.

A man who always gives a woman what she wants will bore that woman. A rich kid who is always used to getting what he wants, will lose appreciation for that something.

This is why intermittent reinforcement is key. So key. You have to make it unknown what will be given, and when. When it comes to attracting men and women with body language, tone of voice and words, you have to be unpredictable. Keep 'em guessing.

Because there's nothing worse, than boring person...

The Altruism Factor – Transcending Mediocrity through Social Capital

But simply manipulating people or trying to subconsciously 'game' people isn't enough. Even if you don't consider these strategies as deception or anything underhanded, they still don't encompass what it takes to succeed. To truly succeed in life, you have to be healthy and happy. And being truly happy and healthy, has to do with relationships.

Research indicates that relationships go very far and reach very wide and penetrate very deeply. In every personal life on this planet, relationships are vital. Literally, vital. You literally need them to live. If you don't have enough, or don't have ones that are meaningful, you will die earlier. You will live painfully. You will feel worse at every turn.

In fact, this is supported by one of the longest-running studies of health and happiness known to man.

The Harvard Study of Adult Development is a longitudinal study that began all the way back in 1938 during the Great Depression. Its aim even then was to discover the psycho-social and biological factors that predicted health and well-being in late life in the 80s and 90s. In tracking the live of

724 men, the study performed annual analyses, featuring everything from questionnaires and interviews on work, home lives and health, to full blood-sample-analyses and even brain scans!

Interestingly, the study used two experimental groups over this long period. The first included sophomores at Harvard College who finished their college careers during WW2, and the second group included boys from some of Boston's poorest areas of the 1930s.

The findings suggested one thing: altruism is good.

Altruism, as the ability to connect and care for others, is apparently so good that it totally changes our lives. As the researchers found, social connections not only had protective effects on the brain, but they led to increased happiness, overall health and lifespan. Being lonely, not having true relationships with others, led to shorter lifespans and a myriad of mental and physical health problems.

The brain functioning of people who didn't feel connected with others drastically declined. They developed more physical impairments at a younger age, and didn't live nearly as long.

Of course, researchers cautioned that 'loneliness' and 'friendship' differed depending upon the person. Simply forcing yourself into friendship or being willing to commit to a person or people isn't enough. You have to hold a true affinity for that individual or group, caring for them selflessly and altruistically, while also feeling that they return that feeling of altruism.

The best relationships, experts state, are warm, equitable, and durable. In other words, you have to be friends with someone you truly like being friends with, the two of you have to feel, and treat each other, like equals, and the two of you must be able to endure the trials and tribulations of life, through thick and thin, and stay friends. Friends with benefits don't count. Many 'friends' on Facebook or social media don't count. A friend who does everything for you without you returning the favor, doesn't count. A friend you bust your hump for who never returns the favor? Doesn't count.

Remember, some people may feel happy just having a boyfriend or girlfriend, husband or wife, and a couple friends. Others may require numerous relationships to feel healthy and happy. Some people may seem like loners, but with just two close friends, will enjoy the protective lifelong benefits. Other people may seem to have tons of friends, but in actuality don't feel connected to any of them, and thus will not enjoy the protective lifelong benefits mentioned in the study.

The researchers even describe the specific cognitive effects of meaningful, altruistic partnerships and friendships. As it turns out, having good friends actually improves your memory. In couples especially, partners who felt they couldn't depend on one another actually experienced a noticeably greater memory decline than couples who did express that bond of trust.

Having lasting relationships, feeling connected, and loving others were the three main powers uncovered in the Harvard study. If you are a person who can truly call a friend a lifelong friend, then you are lucky. Many people go through life, having friends of convenience, or making friends only for so long until life circumstances change. But if you have a partner, a significant other and/or a friend who you will stay with through thick and thin… if your friend lives in another state or country but you still keep the bond strong… if your partner is there for you when life gets tough and doesn't break or flee…

Then *you*, my friend, are in good hands! And your health, body, mind and overall happiness will show it!

Subconscious Priming – How to WIN Friends, Family & All Others

Of course, not all of us can imagine a world of perfect friendship. Some of us have issues we have to sort out. Our families are messed up. Our friends do, and did, things we don't like. We have trust issues. We have attachment problems. We've been hurt before. We're looking for a sign. We feel clueless at times. We feel confident at others. But most times, we feel like we're floating somewhere in the middle.

Life ain't easy. And relationships aren't easier.

If you or someone you know is struggling with these sorts of things (as we all do), then it's time to change. Get your mind and your brain and your heart and soul aligned, by understanding.

Understanding what, you ask?

Well, it all comes down to people. If you can understand the top ways to affect and understand others, you can change your own life for the better. Better yet, you can change *theirs*, by providing *everyone* involved something to gain. So do it. Don't be manipulative, be masterful.

1. Create the Narrative

Everybody does it. We tell a story to entertain guests, we crack jokes, we embellish an anecdote to deliver a message. It happens on T.V. and in commercials, in books and ebooks. On the news and in the media. Everywhere you look, you see narratives. Usually driven by agenda, whether harmless or harmful. And almost always, exploiting your basic human instincts in one form or another.

Truth is, storytelling has been a staple of modern cultures since the beginning of time. Many stories stand the test of time, evolving to new meanings and structures to reflect the changing cultural and societal environments. To appease the changing audiences, with their evolving morals, values, interests and attributes.

If you want to 'prime' someone, storytelling is critical. By 'priming' someone, you are essentially preparing them, subconsciously, for a new age. A new telling. A new agenda. You are setting their minds up so that you can then gear them toward the desired path, thought, feeling, emotion, action and/or behavior of your choosing.

When it comes to the subconscious 'priming' of others, few things are as effective as narratives. In most narratives, there are central themes. These include: overcoming huge adversity (David vs. Goliath), embarking on a journey and returning safely, searching for deeper meaning, going from rags to riches, comedic relief, tragedy, mystery, rebirth of the self or self-realization, and fighting against the Man/establishment/or overruling controller.

These themes are useful for a number of reasons. If you can create a certain narrative, guided by one of these themes, you can implant in a person's head what you want them to believe. If you want somebody to join you in your noble cause, you might spin a narrative of David vs. Goliath, or fighting against the Man. If you want to bring somebody's guard down first, to make them vulnerable, you might spin a narrative of comedic relief. In this case, you may communicate a certain experience that makes light of important things, that focuses on the funny over the serious, and that downplays the person's concerns. If you want to prime someone for changing themselves, you'll spin a narrative of self-rebirth. You may include aspects of powerful celebrities, or rags to riches stories, while ignoring accounts of failure, or of people who never made it out of their tough circumstances.

By using these priming themes, you can effectively create a narrative that omits certain details, includes certain details, and conveys a certain message. Doing this effectively can have profound effects on the human psyche.

Don't believe it?

Just observe the top T.V. shows, movies, and novels of all time. They all inevitably include similar themes. They portray common human struggles and triumphs. They make us identify with the 'good' guys or the 'bad' guys. They make us wake up and take note of our world, our environment, and our own shared realities.

And if you know how to use them, on individuals, groups, or anywhere else – you too, can affect that kind of change.

2. Word Interplay

Change is tied to words. Many words can create meaning by the imagery and sensation they create. Many common phrases carry this power, and are used accordingly in business meetings, seminars, concerts, songs, books – you name it.

Simply consider distinct phrases such as 'drop the ball' or 'killing time' or 'pain in the ass.'

These phrases can be highly effective when used correctly. If somebody is telling you to not 'drop the ball' they create an image of losing grasp, or breaking something, or giving up on holding strong. This usually communicates that you should be tough, and stay consistent, and not give up prematurely. However, if 'drop the ball' is used ineffectively to say, 'drop the ball on the nose,' you might get a strange image. It might seem awkward, it might not makes sense. Maybe it's intended to mean precision or exactitude, but instead it creates a feeling of physical pain or discomfort.

Similarly, the phrase 'killing time' typically means to do something while you wait to get to something else. It basically says, 'let's make time pass.' But what if 'killing time' is intended to mean taking up time? What if somebody says, 'In order to maximize your productivity, killing time is critical' ?

Seems a little off doesn't it? After all, productivity is about making the most of your time. 'Killing time' would seem to imply that you're wasting time or not caring about time, just using it up and tossing it aside like a carcass. You would think, that productivity would want to 'Enliven time' or 'supercharge time' or 'boost time' not *kill* it.

Finally, consider the phrase 'pain in the ass.' Now, we all know what this means. It means something is bothersome, troubling, tough, hard, not fun, not easy to complete, and/or undesirable. But what if you use 'pain in the ass' to signify something good? How do you think that would work? Let's say somebody says, 'Nothing beats a strong pain in the ass.' You might think, *what*? Perhaps, the speaker meant to imply that working hard causes discomfort but it's ultimately good for you. However, given that this phrase is typically associated with another meaning, mostly bad, it's important to not misuse the phrase. Instead of making one want to work harder, the previous speaker would probably only make you think of hemorrhoids or something…

It would be one thing if the speaker compared hard work to a pain in some other part of the body, or a more general pain or 'burn' (often associated with bodybuilding), but the specific words 'pain in the ass' are simply too sensitive and specific for most.

3. Similar but Different

Words have many uses. Ever heard of homophones? Homophones are words that sound the same, are pronounced the same, but are spelled differently, or have different meanings, or are derived from different origins. The reason homophones are so important is because they subtly, but powerfully, hack our subconscious.

Because homophones may sound the same, they carry a double meaning through to our minds. You can basically persuade people without them knowing it. Who knew? See, by applying new words our brains are tricked into receiving stimuli that might have not gone consciously registered. In order to sneak certain meanings into our brains, past our sensory input filters, we have to use a little trickery.

Whether or not your homophone works, depends largely on how you use them. People who are affected may display thoughts or feelings in alignment with what you want. For instance, if you're talking to your one friend who just won something, you might prime him or her a number of ways.

Now stop. Look at the previous sentence. Not the "now stop" sentence, but the one in the previous paragraph. Did you notice how I used "your" and "you're" and "one" and "won"? Those are all homophones. Are you taking about your winning yet? Do you feel like 'the one' because you 'won'?

Okay, so maybe you do and maybe you don't. But the trick of priming isn't some super immediate powerful effect. Not always. Usually, it's about repeated subtle, but suggestive, tactics. Now going back to the previous example. If you're talking to your one friend who just won something…

You could get your friend to talk about himself a lot, or maybe the victory or maybe something else related to the win. Let's say this one person isn't your friend, but somebody you don't like who happened to do well for the team that won. Let's say it was baseball. So you keep talking to this guy or gal, mentioning 'that one' hit or 'the one' at bat or 'who's that one guy?' and so on… You could also mention over and over the word "won" by saying things like, 'You guys really won that one' or 'Still can't believe how well you won' or 'that was one heck of a game' or 'You won it for 'em!'

Now what does this accomplish? Well, there's no telling for certain, but… It might increase this individual's ego to ridiculous levels, it might distract them from other things that happened in the game, or unrelated to the game. It might make this individual more humble.

Using homophones effectively depends upon the individual. You have to experiment and be persistent, but never give up! Homophones can be a very effective way to implant double meaning, focus intensely on a certain meaning, or confuse all meaning for the target of your priming.

4. The Slip-In

One of the best ways to hijack the human mind is through slipping in.

What the heck does that mean?

I'll tell ya. It means slipping in, right at the right moment, when neither right nor left hemisphere of the human brain is activated, right when the target of your 'priming' is stuck in that fraction of unthinking.

This thoughtless void happens to all of us, some more than others (space cadet much?) but it's always there. Sometimes on a brisk run. Sometimes after a long day, during a nice shower, after that first sip of coffee in the morning. It is this thoughtless, mindful state, that the slip-in targets.

By slipping in, we are essentially using a conscious act, big or small, noticeable to more subtle, to disrupt the unconscious processes. The slipping in is the subtle part of the action, which is how your target's subconscious is penetrated. But your conscious act doesn't have to be subtle at all. For instance, you could say a loud curse word. That disrupts the conscious and unconscious, while you then takeover the situation. Maybe you do this to make the person forget his or her train of thought. Maybe you do it so you can then steer the conversation in a different direction. Maybe your choice of curse word is something intentionally embellished, like "son of chain-smoking bitch!" when the person to whom you're talking has a problem with smoking cigarettes.

Whatever your aim, your goal, you can get there by slipping in.

But don't rely on curses or loud intrusions if that's not your style. You can also differentiate your word deliverance. Or frequency. You might say, 'Priming is an effective, even, a highly, highly effective, tactic.' Maybe you stutter your speech or maybe you want to intentionally confuse someone, lull someone into a state of numbness or get them amped, so you speak very quickly without pausing: 'well yea I was worried but who wasn't worried I was using priming which I knew I mean I thought I knew at least for a bit was an effective, even, a highly highly effective, tactic.'

Or… if your intended result is something else, such as getting them to really listen or take you seriously, you '*might. Talk. Like. This. For. Punct-u-at-ed. E-ffect.*' You might also use this when trying to be authoritative or use an embedded command. You could even use a command on yourself, eventually embedding it into your subconscious. Many of us do this unconsciously through feedback loops. We tell ourselves we're worthless then act worthless, reinforcing worthless feelings. By contrast, successful people tell themselves they can *do something* then they *do something*, then they believe even more in their ability to *do something*. But don't be mistaken. I'm not telling you to *be better*, I would never make you *do it* now or *do it* later, even though it is important to be the best version of yourself if you can *do it*.

Embedded commands… see how that worked?

It just comes down to how you work it. The trick is to not be a one-trick pony. Don't overuse the same effects. Employ a variety of 'slip-ins' to disrupt, disturb, exterminate or redirect a persons' train of thoughts, feelings and behaviors. It is an in-the-moment tactic, so if it doesn't work once, there are a millions reasons why. Keep at it, alternate it, and remember that sometimes it might just come down to luck. Saying the right thing at the right time, being at the right place at the right time, catching somebody in the right mood at the perfect time.

Just remember. Whatever you do, do NOT expect the same results from different people. Some people may become totally disrupted, others may be able to continue on with their thoughts, feelings and behaviors like nothing happened. That's just the way it is. Some people are more susceptible to louder more pronounced words. Others are actually more disrupted by softer, harder-to-hear words. And a million other combinations for you to try!

5. Positive Alternatives

This applies to any time when you are trying to persuade someone of positive attributes.

Say you're trying to highlight a product's perks, are trying to sell your own personality traits at a job interview, or are merely flirting in everyday life. When it comes to positive spin, don't use contractions like *'don't.'* Even if you have to say that something or someone is lacking and does not or cannot do something, restructure your phrase.

Instead of saying, 'Don't buy from the fake pretenders'- say: 'Buy from the real experts.' Use an antonym to capture the difference, and contrast a weak word, like pretenders, which denotes weakness of character and values, with a strong word like 'experts', which denotes knowledge and skill.

It's always important to use positive alternatives when you are trying to persuasively communicate or influence. If you want someone to show up on time, instead of saying 'don't get there too late,' say 'get there a little early' or, instead of saying, 'don't do x/y/z again,' say, 'do a/b/c next time.' These constructive, positive, persuasive commands can be very helpful in getting what you want.

Also, a note on product sales. Go to Amazon right now. You might find, no matter the product or product type, that many ad descriptions do one thing. They say something such as,

'Don't waste time with other products' or 'don't buy the hype of others' etc.

Seems good right?

Well, not necessary. See, if these sayings - 'don't buy' or 'don't waste' - are repeated or overemphasized, they can actually lead to reduced sales. Why? Easy. Think about what they've done. They've basically repeated 'don't buy the hype of others' or 'don't waste time with other products'… It's the initial command that gets embedded in a potential customer's mind. So what have you done? You've basically associated the words "don't" "waste" and "buy" with your product. You've associated "don't buy" and "don't waste" with your own product! You've subconsciously told your buyer not to buy or waste time on YOUR product, and whether or not he or she likes it, she is now less likely to buy (and probably doesn't even know why!)

You've primed the wrong thought, and now you've screwed yourself out of a sale!

So next time, prime the right thing, like 'Buy Now' or 'Enjoy yours' or "Relish a new' to get the customer thinking of what will be positively gained, not negatively lost.

Simple enough?

6. Emotive Language

We all get emotional from time to time. And there is no better time to capitalize on those emotions than when 'selling' something. Sell your qualities to a new boss, a new partner, sell your product or services, market and advertise—do what ya gotta do.

But do it well. In order to do it well, you have have have to play on emotions. Pull the heartstrings, stroke the ego, caress them till their warm and fuzzy. Or scare them. Challenge them. Tear them up and build them back bigger, better, and wanting your product like never before.

Use words like *discover unlock optimize activate see find out learn embrace* and other calls-to-action that create a sense of personal development or improvement.

You want the person to feel as though they just need to know what it is you know, or have, or can deliver. People don't buy logically. They buy with emotion. They may justify their buy after the fact, but it is emotion that gets them to make the original purchase.

So use that emotion. Target that emotion. Employ big words, aka highfalutin palaver, in order to change things. If you say, 'this therapy is really good for people with thinking problems,' that communicates one thing. But if you say, 'this psycho-social therapy particularly benefits patients with cognitive deficiencies,' then you are saying something with authority. It's more impressive. It targets that innate emotion in all of us that seeks rational truth and knowledge. It shows greater sense of authority on the subject.

Again, make declarative statements that show you are the leading expert, or the go-to, or the one to know. For instance, statements such as, 'Experts agree' or "Researchers find' or '95% of scientists believe' tend to indicate authority, reason, and indisputable fact.

Use statements that are supported by research, but always—if you can—show why you, your traits, your product or your service, stand out.

7. Inclusiveness

One way to bring people to your side, to prime their thinking for what you're communicating, is to use inclusive language.

Employing universal descriptors is critical to this end. Just think of a lot of ad copy.

You see things like, 'everybody raves' or 'it works for anybody' or 'any condition,' 'anywhere,' 'anytime,' 'good for anything' - while often exaggerated, these universal descriptors represent a critical reality. That life is good and more people are included. It indicates that the product or service is so useful that it can be used by almost anyone.

The reason this works is based on evolutionary psychology. Humans are social creatures. We are born into this world, kept healthy initially be the community (ie; doctors, caretakers, babysitters and parents) and then we are socialized by other groups (educators, employers, friends, etc.).

We are part of a larger tribe—tribalism. We take on aspects of various social groups, because we want to belong. We want to indicate that we're somehow similar, that we can share a unique bond. We have meaning, we have sharing, we have inclusiveness.

What universal descriptors do is *supercharge* that sense of inclusiveness. Suddenly you're part of something global, with a huge population of people. You're important. You're special. And you're part of the all-important club.

This may seem hokey, but used sparingly, it is a powerful persuasive tool.

8. Hit the Switch

Sometimes, you just gotta hit the switch. Say what isn't said, and say what you *do not* want the person to think, feel or do.

Why? Simple. Because it works. Because it catches people off-guard. But more importantly, because it is an easy and cunning way to get people to do what you want. Remember, we're the same people we were when we were younger. When your parents told you to do something, you probably wanted to do it. The lure of underage drinking, why—because it was against the law! Staying out later than curfew, why—because it was fun to do! Doing something considered naughty, or bad, or inappropriate—why? Because you were specifically told *not* to do it, and you want to find out why.

Use this reverse psychology however you want. Maybe you want to get somebody to come with you somewhere. Instead of pleading them to come or accusing them of being a wimp, or boring, or guilt-tripping them, tell them you're fine:

'That's cool, stay here, I know you've got things to do' or 'Don't worry about it, I wanna be alone anyway.'

Play hard ball and call the bluff. If someone isn't giving you the time of day, or getting back to you, or even acknowledging you, simply express 'no biggie, I'm just gonna go ahead and remove you from my contacts.' If somebody is attracted to you, act like you're not interested. Plant the seed in their mind and make them think it was their decision all along.

Reverse psychology acts on that basic impulse that makes humans so amazing, yet also so destructive. Sometimes, we just wanna do what we're told not to. And if you're skilled, you can make what they wanna do, what you wanna do.

You just gotta do it.

9. Vagaries

Believe it or not, there are plenty of perks to being vague. In being vague you are being powerful. Why? Because vagary is about doing what you gotta do to make somebody else feel, uh, something, erh.. somewhere about, uhm, uh… about something.

No, but in all seriousness. Vagary is good. If you're strategically vague, you represent something common to the average person. Take the following example:

At some point your peaks of triumph will meet your lows of failure, and you'll be forced to look deep, down, to make the most and the best of what you've got.

Now what does this mean? Heck, who knows!! It has a general meaning sure, but it will mean something to every person. Each person will look inward and align experiences, feelings, behaviors, attitudes, and thoughts with the statement. One person's moment of triumph was winning a baseball game, another person's was finally purchasing a house. One person's moment of failure was losing a job, another person's might be related to disappointing a friend, or never achieving some dream goal. For every person there will be different aspirations, different goals, and ultimately, a different meaning from the same statement.

It's vague, but it's a good vague. Because it's applicable. It can be sorted out. It can be interpreted.

Now, if you say something like, 'people do stuff that's good and then bad' - how does that work? Sure, it's true. People *do* do things that are good and bad, but the statement is, well, just plain dumb. It doesn't evoke emotion, and if anything it's too simplistic. It's too vague.

So be vague. Just be strategically vague.

Alright, so there ya go. You are living in a world filled with people. These are people you can prime, people you can persuade, people you can change with one word or string of words. These are people you can befriend and understand and influence with the right tactics and strategies.

So don't be a wallflower. Don't sit back and wait for the world to turn for you. Get out there and make the changes you want to see. Be the force you want to be. Actively, intelligently, and consistently use the psychological powers at your disposal to make that change. To force that change. To rearrange the cognitions, feelings and behaviors of those around you, near and far.

It's all possible. It just depends on you, and how far you're willing to go.

Environmental Success: The Top Power Multipliers

So, we've touched briefly on how you can change your environment. One way is by impacting humans. People. By using your interpersonal toolkit to change and correct the relationships you hinge on. But there are also other ways. Better ways, in some respects.

If you're wondering, wonder no more. Transform your environment, and do it with ease and focus. Use your psychology to literally restructure the building blocks of your ecosystem. Sound insane? Sound impossible? Sound highly unlikely? Well it's *not*, and it's not just *not*, it's right. It's the right way, the scientifically-supported, evidence-based, empirical solution to optimizing your environment for success.

It's called Eco-Manipulation

Eco-Manipulation – The Number 1 Way to Transform your environment for Success

If you want to effectively change your environment, you have to do it one step at a time. You have to do it gracefully, not drastically, to see what works and what doesn't. But more than anything, you have to do it in a directed fashion. You have to know what you want, and how to get it. And the number one thing you do for that is this:

Optimize Your Space

It doesn't matter how you define success. Whether it's at work, at home, with family, or out and about. If you have an environment that is conducive to achieving success, your residence, your work office/study, your cubicle, your mom's basement—doesn't matter.

What matters is how you restructure that physical space.

Look at the gurus. They put up motivation posters, they have whiteboards, they have trophies, and weird sculptures, and big quotes, and memorable pictures, and all sorts of reminders of their goals and dreams.

Personalize your space. If you prefer disorganization (linked to creativity) then allow some disorganization. Don't go overboard, but allow some clutter, leave some old trinkets sitting around.

However, if you want productivity and results, you might be more keen to have a clean tidy space. If you're crunching numbers and doing input/output work, a cleaner space is more beneficial. However, if you're creating new projects, combining concepts in new ways, or simply trying to think outside the box, a cluttered, slightly chaotic, slightly disorganized space is what you need.

Put up family photos, pictures of your favorite celebrities, thinkers, athletes and visionaries. Have odd mementos, keep texts and books nearby that only few people understand. If you work a lot, use a comfortable chair and keep a sofa or futon nearby. Have a mini-fridge. Have a stress ball or pinball machine or video game console. Make sure to allow enough space between your primary work space (a desk or table) and the 'fun stuff' in the room.

Stay hydrated, have snacks on deck, and make sure you are attuned to what you're doing.

Also be sure to reduce distractions. Now, some people might find music distracting, others find a soft beat useful as a backdrop for your thoughts. Some people simply need music to initiate work. Others can't get a thing done with it.

Make sure where ever you are, whatever you're doing, you allow only those distractions that you can handle. Use softer lighting, but not too soft to make you sleepy. Use a headphone if you want to 'zone' in. Make sure your 'space' is away from people who may be obnoxious or distracting. Find a time and a place that is ideal for you.

Put your phone away. Put your social media away. Don't open too many tabs on your computer. And don't be afraid of, again, a little water and snack. In fact, research indicates that having something to sip on is ideal for boosting productivity. Think of it this way. When you have something to drink periodically, you have a built-in, natural excuse for a break. You can work for 15 minutes, then take a sip, pause, review, and then get back to work. You have something to naturally break up the workload into successive segments that are neither too long nor too overwhelming.

Make your task manageable by having some snacks nearby. Incentivize. Tell yourself you won't crack that soda or bag of chips until you get x/y/z done. Allow yourself brief breaks, a place to walk. It is important that wherever you are, you can walk. You need to be able to move quickly and easily when your brain goes blank and you feel all riled up and constricted.

Just walking for 10 minutes at a time has been shown to clear the head and reinvigorate the brain.

Another way to optimize your environment is by incentivizing desired behaviors at every turn. This can be done a number of ways. The best way, arguably, is through locus optimizing. You optimize a locus when you make a specific, small and functional environment even more functional.

Say for instance, you want to achieve more in your office. So you leave a laptop there, or you keep certain duplicates of files that normally you have at home. Or maybe you have post-its telling you what to do. At home, you could do something similar. You could have reminder notices on the fridge, in a cabinet, on the T.V., anywhere that you frequent.

You may leave certain important websites open on your laptop or computer, or as your homepage. You could have a different homepage for Google Chrome, or Internet Explorer or Mozilla.

But may this has nothing to do with work productivity. Maybe you want to optimize other loci for overall holistic success. So whaddaya do? Well, you leave a toothbrush in the shower or at work. You put various unrelated items near one another to remind you do something.

You schedule your average day so locations of importance are nearby. You find an inexpensive grocery store with items you want that is equi-distant from work and home. You find a convenient gym to start your membership. You find local extracurricular and sports clubs for the kids that aren't too far, in community fields or centers relatively close. You find convenient bike and running trails, hiking sites, outdoor recreational spots, that are nearby.

So in the end, what happens? Easy, you get healthy, you stay motivated, you get the products and services you want, and—of course—you save on gas! The bottom line is having a disciplined, practical approach to achieving your goals. There are only 24 hours in a day, and most of us are lacking sleep as is! So what you wanna do is make the most of your waking hours.

Become the person who 'has it figured out.' Not only will you be the envy of others, but you'll more importantly, serve as a role model and positive example for those just like you. That is, like-minded people who want to make the most of themselves by also making the most of the worlds in which they thrive.

Remember: you are also the company you keep. You have to find the environment you want to be a part of, then you have to make it the environment you can never be apart *from*. If you want to be a lawyer, hang around with established lawyers. If you want to one day have a family, hang with couples with kids. If you're an aspiring artist, hang with artists.

Some experts contend that we are the average of the 5 people we spend the most time with. If you aren't spending time with 5 people, branch out! Get out of your bubble or echochamber! Meet people who have already done what you want to do. But make sure they're not the same. You want different people of different genders, races, creeds and politics. Your best and closest friends can be otherwise, but when it comes to hanging with people who are geared toward career success… You want a tight niche! All similar in one major way, all different in nuanced ways within that major way.

Be patient. With the right networking, you'll get there and faster than you ever thought possible! That is, if people and environment are even enough...

The Schema Loop – How to Harness the Power of the Psycho-Physical

Sometimes people and environment aren't enough. And that's where schema comes in.

What's a schema, you ask?

<u>Schema Theory</u> is a major discipline in cognitive psychology that has been evolving and expanding in fascinating ways for a number of decades. A schema is essentially an organizing perceptual framework of the human mind. It can also be described as a higher-order cognitive structure that sets the foundation for all sorts of human knowledge and skills. One's schema or schemata provide an explanation for how old and new knowledge interact to impact perception, language, thought, and memory. The original theory of schemata was Bartlett's Schema Theory (1932) which defined these cognoscenti structures as actively organized from past reactions and experiences to inform an adaptive organic response in a living organism. Bartlett thought that schemata were unconscious structures, active but not consciously aware. He believed that our past experiences, and everything tied to them, created an unconscious mass wherein the totality was greater than the sum of its parts.

Basically, what Bartlett was getting at was this: when you experience enough *things*, you form a general cognitive representation. And this applies to anything. For instance, your experiences with people, you can fall on a spectrum from absolutely hating them to absolutely loving them. You can think certain types are evil or tough or wrong or immoral or contemptuous or elitist or simple or dumb or genius and on and on and on…

Bartlett believed that all old information represented in the schema interacted with new information to actively create a finely-tuned, always subtly-changing schema. So based on past experience and new experience, your organization framework for the world could change totally or stay the same. For instance, you might believe that roller coasters are safe. This was based on your own personal experiences and the information you had garnered in the past. However, after experiencing a near-death event on a roller coaster, you might no longer believe roller coasters are safe at all, even if hard data indicated the likelihood of such an event was insignificant.

Of course, what Barlett also tapped into was the idea of confirmation bias. Confirmation bias means that we basically seek out, learn and understand information according to our preconceived beliefs about the world. One person might see one thing, and another person might see the same exact thing. Yet both people could come to totally different conclusions. One polar example of this is politics, in which one side may seek only evidence that confirms its bias, while the other side seeks only evidence that confirms its bias. In the end, both sides never find compromise or middle-ground.

Bartlett conducted a number of experiments to test this. One required participants to read a bunch of material and then complete an exam to show recall capability. Bartlett found that participants made many meaningful errors in a systematic way, in accordance with old information and beliefs. For instance one person might know all about one baseball team and love the team, based on good player stats, and the teams' history of good stats. When presented with new information, showing negative stats in the players and team's history, that same person might find it hard to square this information with the overriding belief that the baseball team is flawless. Thus, when asked to recall this new information, the person might selectively forget or not recall information highlighting the negative stats of the team, while still remembering many of the good stats from earlier.

In fact, Barlett used sports players as evidence of schemata. He argued that many experienced, talented players will be better at adjusting to new patterns or plays in their sport than less experienced, less talented players. Thus, Barlett argued that these players are not unconsciously recalling fixed motor movements and skill-sets, but adaptive, generalized schemata.

Since Barlett's theorizing and hypothesis-testing of schemata, modern researchers have taken the reins. Many researchers today now agree that although schemata may be derived from smaller mental structures, they are still qualitatively different than those structures combined. Just like chemical interactions create structurally different compounds, the interactions of smaller cognitive structures create larger, new schemata. This is called the *emergent levels theory* of schemata, which supposes that the groupings of basic mental atoms create qualitatively different, larger levels upon levels upon levels, leading to the largest organizational structure of the schema.

But let's pause. If all of this is getting tedious or too theoretical, remember this: You are your schema. Moreover, your reality is your schema. If you want to change your world and your reality, for the worst, the best, or something in between, you have to chance your schema.

But this is no easy task. It starts with basic exercises, but must encompass all aspects of your life, in your every mental process connected to this world. Take for instance the broadest conception of schemata. Schemata can be conceived of as structures that organize your perceptual framework of Life, right? So, what this means is that there can be an infinite number of ways you can broadly see the world, and then interpret, the innumerable events within that world, as they relate to you and to other people, places and things.

So let's simplify. Let's take one hotly-debated topic, which is the debate between religious individuals and non-religious individuals. Theists vs atheists.

Okay.

So think about this in terms of schemata. A highly religious, devout Christian will see the world as indicative of God, as a product or representation or gift or creation of God. God's work and the hand of God will be conceived in a number of ways. Meanwhile, the atheist will not see these things through the lens of God's work. The atheist will argue that things that happen have nothing to do with God.

Now let's take it further. Say the religious person has a son. That son gets robbed and shot in the head. The son is rushed to the E.R. and the son's chances of survival are next-to-none. Incredibly, the son survives and goes on to make a full recovery without lasting brain damage.

Now, say the same thing happens to the atheist's son.

The two highly divergent schemata of the atheist and the theist will bring totally different meanings to the same event. For the devout Christian, the recovery is considered miraculous. God blessed his or her son, and his or her family, and the devout Christian will move forward in the world more assured of God's presence than ever before. He or she might even become more devoted, giving more to charity, and getting more personally involved with groups helping families suffering from loss and tragedy due to violent robberies.

Now, the atheist will view the recovery as extremely rare, as a near statistical improbability. The atheist will credit all sorts of factors, such as timing, the doctors and nurses in the

E.R., and his or her son's personal ability/genetics/strength to overcome. Luck will also be acknowledged, in that if the bullet had been just an inch the other way, it would have been fatal.

Now, the devout Christian might acknowledge all these factors too. However, the devout Christian will likely credit these many incredible factors to God's intervention, to prayer, to a higher purpose. The atheist, by contrast, will not. The atheist, like the Christian, may still move onto the world feeling better and more positive, giving to charities and getting personally involved with groups helping families, but the atheist will not attribute these new developments to God.

So what do we have? We have two different people with two totally different schemata. The Christian has mentally organized the many facets of the world as somehow related to God, the atheist has organized the many facets of the world as somehow related to things other than God.

But this is just one example. And labeling schemata gets difficult. For instance, the Christian might also be a scientist, who views things as tied to a higher power not yet within the realm of human empirical study. The atheist might be an artist or writer, who ascribes meaning to some demonstrable but subtle energy between all things. The atheist will say that this energy is merely a series of highly complicated electro-chemical impulses; the Christian, by contrast, may see this incredible energy as too profound to be anything but the presence and power of God.

In the end, our schemata can overlap and counteract new information or skew new information or misrepresent or remove new information. We may also remove old information or falsely remember old information when new information is too compelling.

All of these processes and mechanisms, unconscious and conscious, impact the way we perceive, and act within, the world. And that world, no matter what we do, is amazing.

So don't fall victim to fear or insecurity. If you want to change your schemata, start by changing how you think about the most basic events. Seek the truth over bias, and expose yourself to paradigm-shattering information. Be open-minded, divorced from ideology, tied to reality. Mix with new people, see new things, and absorb new experiences. Never stop questioning, and never stop fashioning, yourself and your reality as you see it.

Go into the World and Apply your Quotient for Success. Apply it, Do it, and WIN BIG Today.

No matter how you define success, we can all agree... It's something good. It is something that gives us purpose and propels us out of bed in the morning and back in bed at night. A reason to sleep, awaken, and keep on trucking. A reason to go after that which we crave most, to achieve that which we need the deepest. We are human, we are flawed, and we are incredibly complicated.

But the one thing we are not, is weak.

So step up. Apply the science taught in this introduction here, and become the Powerhouse you've always wanted to be. In all the myriad ways, with all the myriad powers, you've wanted to have.

A Special Note:

Thank you for reading *"The Success Quotient: How to Capitalize on YOUR OWN Hidden Formula"* If you enjoyed reading this book and would like to be included on an email list for when similar content is available, feel free:

<u>SUBSCRIBE</u>

As always, thank you for reading. And may you continue to live healthily and happily.

Sincerely,

<u>C.K. Murray</u>

Other works by C.K. Murray:

1. <u>*Mindfulness Explained: The Mindful Solution to Stress, Depression, and Chronic Unhappiness*</u>

2. <u>*Emotional Intelligence Explained: How to Master Emotional Intelligence and Unlock Your True Ability*</u>

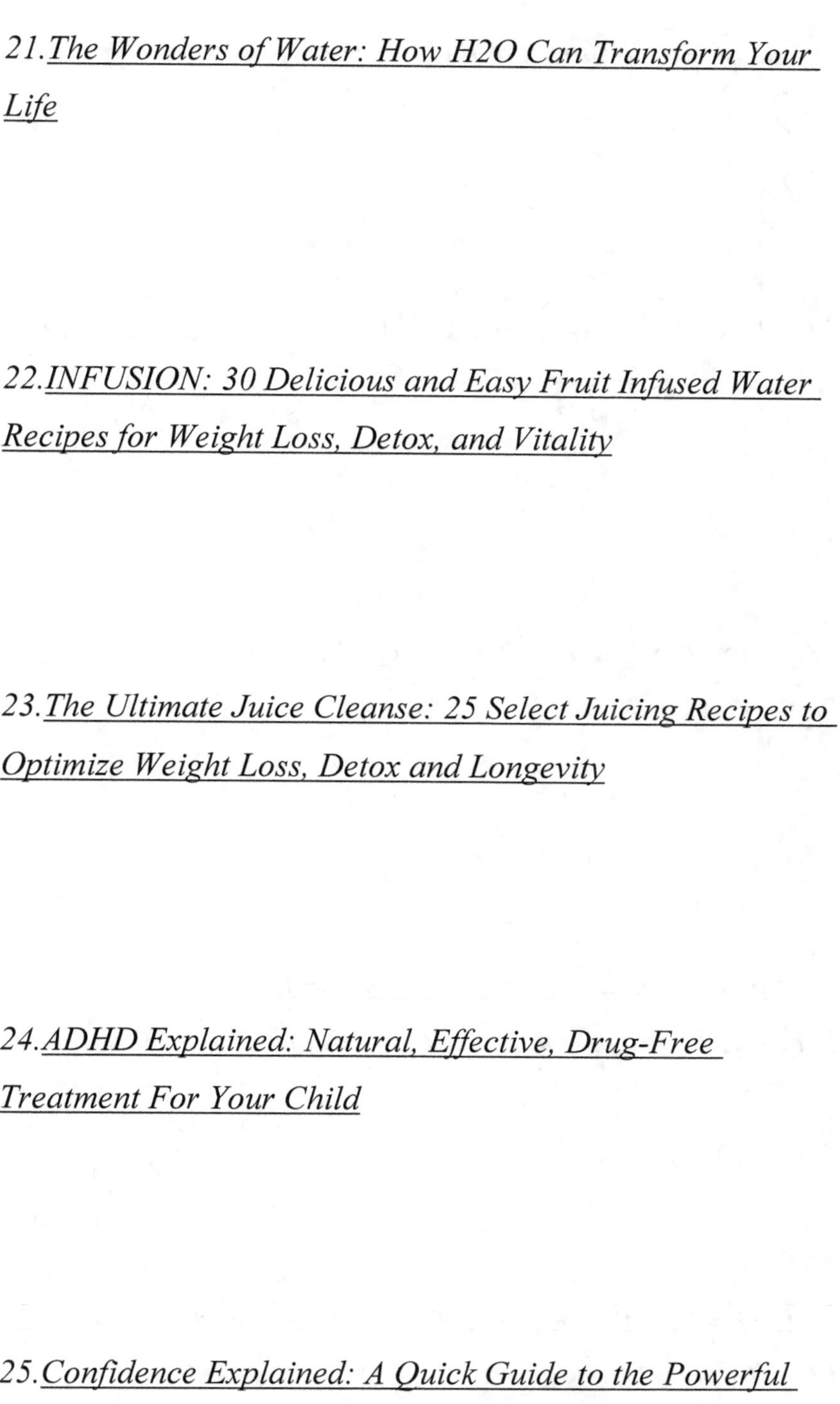

www.ingramcontent.com/pod-product-compliance
Lightning Source LLC
Chambersburg PA
CBHW070119260726
48658CB00001B/175

* 9 7 8 1 7 2 2 4 3 7 6 0 2 *